# A Guide to
# Hawk Watching
# in North America

Donald S. Heintzelman

 Keystone Books

The Pennsylvania State University Press
University Park and London

*For Robert and Anne MacClay*

All photographs are by the author unless another source is credited by initials. A full acknowledgment of the sources of the photographs and artwork appears in the Preface.

Library of Congress Cataloging in Publication Data
Heintzelman, Donald S
   A guide to hawk watching in North America.
   Includes bibliography and index.
   1.   Birds of prey—North America.   2.   Bird watching—
North America.   I.   Title.   II.   Title: Hawk watching
in North America.
QL696.F3H46         598.9'1         78-21003
ISBN 0-271-00212-3

Printed in the United States of America

# Contents

# Checklist of North American Hawks

( )    Turkey Vulture
( )    Black Vulture
( )    California Condor
( )    Osprey
( )    White-tailed Kite
( )    Swallow-tailed Kite
( )    Hook-billed Kite
( )    Mississippi Kite
( )    Snail (Everglade) Kite
( )    Northern Goshawk
( )    Sharp-shinned Hawk
( )    Cooper's Hawk
( )    Red-tailed Hawk
( )    Red-shouldered Hawk
( )    Broad-winged Hawk
( )    Short-tailed Hawk
( )    Swainson's Hawk
( )    Zone-tailed Hawk
( )    White-tailed Hawk
( )    Rough-legged Hawk
( )    Ferruginous Hawk
( )    Gray Hawk
( )    Harris' Hawk
( )    Common Black Hawk
( )    Golden Eagle
( )    Bald Eagle
( )    White-tailed Eagle
( )    Northern Harrier (Marsh Hawk)
( )    Crested Caracara
( )    Gyrfalcon
( )    Prairie Falcon
( )    Peregrine Falcon
( )    Aplomado Falcon
( )    Merlin
( )    American Kestrel (Sparrow Hawk)

# Preface

Increasing interest in diurnal birds of prey in recent years by raptor biologists, conservationists, and recreational hawk watchers precipitated the need for a compact North American hawk-watching field guide that would provide more comprehensive and detailed information about the observation, identification, biology, and ecology of diurnal raptors than is traditionally included in the standard field guides to bird identification.

This guide aims to give that basic information. The raptor biologist will find the text and illustrations useful while conducting field studies. Raptor conservationists will also find the guide a valuable conservation-education tool to be used on behalf of the protection, preservation, and appreciation of North American diurnal birds of prey. Finally recreational hawk watchers, and birders generally, will find the guide helpful as they strive to enjoy their hobby.

In recent years recreational hawk watching has become a popular form of bird watching—and for good reason. Most hawks, eagles, and falcons are large, powerful, and spectacular. The sight of any of these birds is a memorable experience for every birder. Hence a visit to one of the excellent hawk lookouts in the United States or Canada is always a noteworthy event during the spring and autumn migration seasons. Indeed large numbers of birders now plan special field trips to these lookouts hoping to see numerous Broad-winged, Sharp-shinned, or Red-tailed Hawks. Some enthusiasts visit the best lookouts weekend after weekend, eagerly watching for rare and spectacular birds such as Golden Eagles, Bald Eagles, and Peregrine Falcons. These birders know that hawk watching requires persistence; one must be willing to spend long hours on the lookouts. But the results are worthwhile, and thousands of people have enjoyed their first views of eagles or other rare species after such tireless vigils. Do not despair if you are disappointed on your first trip. Even experts sometimes predict good hawk flights at the eastern lookouts and are disappointed. Experienced hawk watchers have a favorite expression: "You should have been here yesterday!"

Watching hawks and other diurnal raptors, however, is not restricted to visits to hawk-migration lookouts. There are other worthwhile places where one can expect to see some of these birds. In California, for example, several special observation points are maintained for persons wishing to see endangered California Condors. In Idaho the Snake River Birds of Prey Natural Area offers unique raptor-viewing opportunities at possibly the most dense concentration of nesting raptors in North America. In Florida there are still a few spots where one may observe the endangered North American subspecies of the Snail Kite. In the Southwest and elsewhere roadside raptor viewing can be very worthwhile. Along the upper Mississippi River and other places large numbers of wintering Bald Eagles can be observed from safe distances without disturbing the birds. Clearly, one can enjoy hawk watching during any season of the year at the proper location.

In 1972 an early edition of this guide was published under the title *A Guide to Northeastern Hawk Watching*. In 1973 it was followed by the completion of *Autumn Hawk Flights* (Rutgers University Press, 1975) which compiled, organized, and summarized the considerable volume of published and unpublished information on hawk migrations in eastern North America up to that time. In 1976 *A Guide to Eastern Hawk Watching* was published in a pocket-size format. The guide provided brief species descriptions, a large selection of photographs of diurnal raptors in overhead flight positions, descriptions and directions for visiting dozens of hawk-migration lookouts in the East, and other information.

At the time of publication of the eastern guide the rich diurnal raptor fauna of western North America was neglected because not enough information was available on western raptor viewing to justify inclusion of the West in the guide. That situation has changed to some extent due to the activities of the Hawk Migration Association of North America, the Southwest Hawk Watch, and various independent observers. Furthermore, a greater number of photographs of western diurnal raptors are now available than in the past thus allowing the use of good photographic illustrations. The time was certainly ripe for the preparation of this guide.

The revisions and additions to the eastern hawk-watching guide are extensive in order to make this volume as complete and comprehensive as possible. Among the books that were consulted in addition to the previously mentioned texts are: the American Birding Association's *A. B. A. Checklist: Birds of Continental United States and Canada*, the American Ornithologists' Union's *Check-List of North American Birds* (Fifth Edition and Supplements), Bailey and Niedrach's *Birds of Colorado*, Bent's *Life Histories of North American Birds of Prey*, Berger's *Hawaiian Birdlife*, Brett and Nagy's *Feathers in the Wind*, Broun's *Hawks Aloft*, Brown and Amadon's *Eagles, Hawks and Falcons of the World*, Bruun and Singer's *Birds of Europe*, Bull and Farrand's *The Audubon Society Field Guide to North American Birds*, Chancellor's *World Conference on Birds of Prey: Report of Proceedings Vienna 1975*, Cruickshank's *Bird Islands Down East*, Friedmann's *The Birds of North and Middle America* (Part XI),

Gabrielson and Lincoln's *The Birds of Alaska*, Harrison's *A Field Guide to Birds' Nests*, Heinzel, Fitter, and Parslow's *The Birds of Britain and Europe with North Africa and the Middle East*, Imhof's *Alabama Birds*, Koford's *The California Condor*, Lowery's *Louisiana Birds*, May's *The Hawks of North America*, McMillan's *Man and the California Condor*, Meng's "The Cooper's Hawk" (Ph.D. dissertation), Mengel's *The Birds of Kentucky*, Miller, McMillan, and McMillan's *The Current Status and Welfare of the California Condor*, Oberholser and Kincaid's *The Bird Life of Texas*, Ogden's *Transactions of the North American Osprey Research Conference*, Peterson's *A Field Guide to the Birds*, *A Field Guide to Western Birds*, and *A Field Guide to the Birds of Texas*, Peterson and Chalif's *A Field Guide to Mexican Birds and Adjacent Central America*, Peterson, Mountfort, and Hollom's *A Field Guide to the Birds of Britain and Europe*, Pettingill's *A Guide to Bird Finding East of the Mississippi*, Porter, Willis, Christensen, and Nielsen's *Flight Identification of European Raptors*, Pough's *Audubon Water Bird Guide: Water, Game, and Large Land Birds*, Robards and Taylow's *Bald Eagles in Alaska*, Robbins and Singer's *Birds of North America*, Spencer's *Wintering of the Migrant Bald Eagle in the Lower 48 States*, Spofford's *The Golden Eagle in the Trans-Pecos and Edwards Plateau of Texas*, Stieglitz and Thompson's *Status and Life History of the Everglade Kite in the United States*, Stone's *Bird Studies at Old Cape May*, Swann's *A Monograph of the Birds of Prey*, Watson's *The Hen Harrier*, and Wilbur's *The California Condor, 1966–76*.

Valuable information was also extracted from periodicals, particularly from files of *American Biology Teacher, American Birds, Atlantic Naturalist, Audubon, Audubon Bulletin, Audubon Leader, Auk, Birding, Birding News Survey, Bird Observer of Eastern Massachusetts, Bulletin Massachusetts Audubon Society, Bulletin Natural History Society of Maryland, California Condor, California Fish and Game, Cassinia, Cleveland Bird Calendar, Condor, Delaware Conservationist, Eagle Valley News, Elepaio, EBBA News, Endangered Species Technical Bulletin, Hawk Mountain News, Jack-Pine Warbler, Journal Hawk Migration Association North America, Journal Wildlife Management, Kingbird, Living Bird, Maryland Birdlife, Migrant, New Jersey Audubon, New Jersey Nature News, New Jersey State Museum Science Notes, New Mexico Ornithological Society Bulletin, Newsletter Hawk Migration Association North America, Raptor Research News, Redstart, Search, Southwest Hawk Watch Newsletter, Urner Field Observer, Virginia Society of Ornithology Newsletter, Washington Wildlife,* and the *Wilson Bulletin.*

To make a uniform evaluation of the importance of hawk-migration lookouts, data from each lookout were compared with one of the following rating scales. Hawk counts from Hawk Mountain Sanctuary, Pennsylvania, provided the baseline data from which the two scales were prepared. Whenever possible I used the average number of hawks observed per hour to evaluate and rate a site. If that information was unavailable, I used the average number of hawks observed per day. In some instances neither of these data was available. Then I used my judgment, rooted in a quarter century of field experience studying hawk migrations, to arrive at a site's rating.

## Hawks Per Hour Rating Scale

| Lookout Rating | Average Number of Hawks Observed Per Hour |
|---|---|
| Poor | 0 to 11 |
| Fair | 12 to 22 |
| Good | 23 to 33 |
| Excellent | 34 or more |

## Hawks Per Day Rating Scale

| Lookout Rating | Average Number of Hawks Observed Per Day |
|---|---|
| Poor | 0 to 46 |
| Fair | 47 to 92 |
| Good | 93 to 138 |
| Excellent | 139 or more |

A number of persons provided valuable information or assistance during the preparation of this guide or one of its earlier versions. Dean Amadon and Laurence C. Binford read an early draft of the species accounts and made helpful comments and recommendations. John Borneman, Eben McMillan, and Sanford R. Wilbur provided much information and helpful comments on the California Condor. Dean P. Hector provided valuable comments on the Aplomado Falcon, and Heinz Meng suggested improvements on the accipiter and Peregrine Falcon species accounts. The following persons also provided helpful information: Jackson B. Abbott, Wayne D. Adams, Stanton Allaben, J. C. Appel, G. N. Appell, Henry Armistead, Katherine Balderston, Moreton R. Bates, Michael Bennett, Andrew J. Berger, Richard C. Bollinger, Martin Borko, Norman Bowers, Maurice Brooks, H. Meade Cadot, Jr., Ray Chandler, Philip Conroy, Rena Cote, Neil Currie, Charles R. Darling, Tom Davis, Russell E. Dickenson, Robert and Lucy Duncan, Elton Fawks, Carl L. Garner, Jay George, Bill Ginn, Michael P. Gooley, Michel Gosselin, Curtice Griffin, William N. Grigg, John A. Guthrie, Theodore R. Hake, David Hancock, Greg Hanisek, Daniel R. Heathcote, Neil Henderson, Gerald J. Hennessey, John D. Hill, Maurice E. Hobaugh, Stephen W. Hoffman, Edwin H. Horning, Lynn C. Howard, John P. Hubbard, Thomas A. Imhof, Terrence N. Ingram, Paul Jeheber, M. Alan Jenkins, Alice H. Kelley, William A. Klamm, D. L. Knohr,

Rodney Krey, Carol Kruse, Edward J. Kurtz, David S. Lee, Robert and Anne MacClay, William Marx, Paul McCary, Leslie C. McDowell, Terrence P. McEneaney, Donald E. McKnight, Alfred and Barbara Merritt, George Momberger, Myriam P. Moore, Kenneth O. Morgan, Melvin T. Nail, Belle Peebles, John P. Perkins, Elizabeth W. Phinney, Alan Pistorius, Peggy Powell, Noble S. Proctor, Jan Reese, Tudor Richards, Paul M. Roberts, D. M. Ross, John H. Rufli, David Schwenker, Fred Scott, John Serrao, Wayne A. Shifflett, Anne Shreve, Robert W. Smart, Daniel Smiley, T. Paul Smith, Bradley Snyder, Stephen J. Stedman, Karen Steenhof, Jim Stevenson, Mary Ann Sunderlin, Milton B. Suthers, John E. Swedberg, Martha F. Sykes, Herbert G. Troester, F. Prescott Ward, John E. Warnock, Albert S. Watson, Arthur S. Weaver, Ken Wiley, and Gus Yaki.

Photographs are an important part of this guide, and I used my own whenever possible. Additional photographs were provided by various agencies, institutions, and individuals including the Glacier National Park, Massachusetts Division of Fisheries and Wildlife, National Park Service, San Diego Zoo, United States Fish and Wildlife Service, United States Forest Service, John C. Arvin, William F. Braerman, Bill Byrne, Allan D. Cruickshank, Helen Cruickshank, Ray C. Erickson, Hal Flanders, Jim Frates, Frikrik R. Fridriksson, Karl-Erik Fridzén, Harry Goldman, Dean P. Hector, Eric Hosking, Dustin Huntington, M. Alan Jenkins, Carl B. Koford, William C. Krantz, Karl L. Maslowski, Eben McMillan, Heinz Meng, Willis Peterson, Ray Quigley, Ron Quigley, Fred Sibley, Barton M. Snyder, Bruce A. Sorrie, Jan Sosik, Walter R. Spofford, Jack Swedberg, Tommy Swindell, Fred Tilly, Bobby Tulloch, Sanford R. Wilbur, and Dale and Marian Zimmerman.

The drawings of various species were prepared for use in this guide by Rod Arbogast. Some of the field data forms reproduced in Appendix 4 are printed with the permission of Andrew Bihun, Jr., of the Montclair Bird Club, and James J. Brett, of the Hawk Mountain Sanctuary Association.

The task of preparing A Guide to Hawk Watching in North America has been complex and enormous. I would like to express my appreciation to each of the persons who assisted in one way or another in this conservation-education effort on behalf of diurnal birds of prey in North America.

Allentown, Pa.                                    Donald S. Heintzelman
15 August 1978

# List of Abbreviations

Frequently cited sources in the Reference sections of Hawk Migration Lookouts and Bald Eagle Viewing Areas are abbreviated as follows:

AB      *Audubon Bulletin*
AHF     *Autumn Hawk Flights* (Rutgers University Press, 1975)
BEA     *Bald Eagles in Alaska* (U.S. Departments of Interior and Agriculture, no date)
GBF     *A Guide to Bird Finding East of the Mississippi* (Oxford University Press, 1977)
GEHW    *A Guide to Eastern Hawk Watching* (Pennsylvania State University Press, 1976)
JHMA    *Journal Hawk Migration Assn. North America*
NHMA    *Newsletter Hawk Migration Assn. North America*
WBMR    *Winter Birding along the Mississippi River* (Eagle Valley Environmentalists, Inc., no date)
WMBE    *Wintering of the Migrant Bald Eagle in the Lower 48 States* (National Agricultural Chemicals Association, 1976)

# Species Accounts

## New World Vultures: Cathartidae

Vultures are large black or dark brown carrion-eating birds. The Turkey Vulture is widespread, the Black Vulture less so. One species, the California Condor, is near extinction (40 or less survive) and is restricted to a small area of California.

### Turkey Vulture *Cathartes aura*

**Wingspread:** 68 to 72 inches (172 to 182 centimeters).
**Length:** 26 to 32 inches (66 to 81 centimeters).
**Field Recognition:** *Adult (sexes similar)*—Large, nearly eagle-size dark brown bird; appears black at a distance. Wings grayish or silvery on undersides of primaries and secondaries, giving bird a two-toned appearance. Wings held in a V or dihedral when bird is in flight. Head frequently pointed down rather than extending forward. Tail relatively long, extending well beyond rear edge of wings; tip normally rounded but sometimes damaged. Naked head reddish-crimson with short blackish bristles visible only at very close range. Eyes grayish-brown; bill ivory white; cere red; legs and feet fleshy-whitish. *Immature (sexes similar)*—Similar to adults, but naked head grayish-black. In some recently fledged birds ring of white down still circles base of neck. Bill black. *Chick*—Covered with white natal down; head naked and dark as in immature.
**Flight Style:** Tilts from side to side when soaring. Occasional wingbeats deep and powerful but appear labored.
**Voice:** Various hisses and grunts when bird is cornered; otherwise silent.
**Nest:** None constructed. Eggs deposited on the ground, sometimes on leaf or other litter, in caves, cliffs, hollow logs, and similar protected places.
**Eggs:** 2 (rarely 1 or 3) dull or creamy white with brown blotches. Incubation period about 40 days.
**Food:** Carrion (especially small animals); rarely rotting fruits or vegetables.
**Habitat:** Widespread in open country. Perches on posts, tall dead trees, electric wires, fences, and on or near dead animals on the ground.
**Range:** Southern Canada south to Tierra del Fuego.

# Black Vulture *Coragyps atratus*

**Wingspread:** 54 to 60 inches (137 to 152 centimeters).
**Length:** 23 to 27 inches (58 to 68 centimeters).
**Field Recognition:** *Adult (sexes similar)*—Large black bird with whitish patch on underside of each wing near the tip. Tail short, barely extending beyond rear edge of wings; tip square. Naked head blackish-gray; neck more or less corrugated. Eyes, legs, and feet dark brown; bill brownish-black with lighter tip. *Immature (sexes similar)*—Similar to adult but plumage duller and neck not corrugated. *Chick*—Covered with thick buffy (not white) natal down. Naked head similar to immature.
**Flight Style:** Several flaps, then short sail. Generally soars less than Turkey Vulture, but when soaring tends to reach higher altitudes than Turkey Vulture.
**Voice:** Variety of hissing, rasping snarls when cornered; otherwise silent.
**Nest:** None constructed. Eggs deposited on the ground, on leaves or other litter, in caves, hollow stumps, hollow logs, on bare ground underneath tangles of vines, or other protected places.

*Black Vulture nest and eggs.*

**Eggs:** 2 (rarely 1 or 3) pale gray-green with few dark brown blotches. Incubation period 28 to 39 days (28 to 30 days in Florida).

**Food:** Carrion. Rarely kills young or injured animals, domestic or wild; known to eat rotting fruit or vegetables at times.

**Habitat:** Much the same as for Turkey Vulture, except not occurring at higher elevations. Sometimes gathers in large numbers to feed upon carrion.

**Range:** Southern United States south to Chile and Argentina; also Trinidad. Occasionally wanders into more northern states; now breeding in Pennsylvania.

## California Condor *Gymnogyps californianus*

**Wingspread:** 8½ to 9½ feet (2.6 to 2.8 meters).

**Length:** 43 to 55 inches (109 to 139 centimeters).

**Field Recognition:** Huge. Subtle changes occur continually in condor's plumage until it reaches adult stage, resulting in too much variation in developmental plumage to allow precise determination of age. Birds sometimes can be placed in one of following approximate age classes adapted from Koford (*The California Condor,* 1953) and Wilbur (*California Fish and Game,* 1975, 61:144–48) although not all may fall exactly into any one category. *Adult (sixth year or older)*—Black with orange or yellow head and neck; pure white underwing coverts. *Sub-adult (fourth and fifth year)*—Black, head sooty with well-defined ring of pale pink skin on neck of early fourth-year birds (so-called ring-necked birds); exact age at which pink ring begins to appear and progress outward until entire neck is pink and head changes to orange is somewhat variable, but transition may begin toward end of third year. By late fourth or early fifth year, neck is entirely pink. Underwing coverts white, more or less similar to adults', but have distinctive dark patch in center of white near body. Difficulty in distinguishing this plumage from that of some immatures at a distance or in unfavorable light leads some experienced condor observers to refer to sub-adults and early immatures as "light immature" birds. *Immature (first to third year)*—Considerable variability in plumage patterns makes it difficult, and sometimes impossible, to determine accurately precise age of birds in this age class. However, second- and third-year birds are black with grayish heads. Eyes red (in good light at a close distance). In many birds underwing coverts mostly tawny or brown (so-called dark immature birds) rather than mottled white. (Several captive birds had underwing coverts mottled with much white and some brown but no typical "dark" stage; reason for discrepancy unknown.) Later in immature stage, perhaps late in third year, "ring-necked" plumage begins to appear as transition into difficult-to-recognize sub-adult plumage. First-year birds best recognized by erratic flight rather than plumage although they are black with gray head and neck but no "ring-necked" feature of older birds. Eyes brown. Underwing coverts white, irregularly mottled with brown, having distinctive dark patch in center near body giving birds an appearance deceptively similar to sub-adult condors. Some experienced condor observers refer to these birds as "light immature" condors. When soaring, tip of tail slightly pointed rather than smoothly rounded as in adults. *Chick*—Covered with white natal down changing at about 20 days to dark gray down. At about 55 days black juvenal plumage begins to appear. By about 30 weeks most of juvenal (first-year) plumage is in place. Head naked.

**Flight Style:** Soars for hours on broad, flat wings (almost airplane-like) without rocking and tilting exhibited by smaller Turkey Vulture in areas inhabited by condors. Golden Eagles also occur in areas inhabited by condors but are smaller. In head-on or rear views condor's primaries appear brush-like at tips. Soaring condors frequently flex wings upward about 90 degrees then backward about 45 degrees at wrists in so-called double dip, requiring one to two seconds to complete (slower than in other raptors) before continuing normal soaring activity. Purpose of double dip is to increase speed, lose elevation, or avoid stall; as many as 26 consecutive double dips seen within 5- to 15-second intervals when condor flew into strong wind. Not infrequently soaring condors produce "steady hissing whistle" due to action of air upon wings. Whistle sometimes audible up to distances of 100 yards (90 meters). Other styles of flight, including flex-gliding and flapping, also used. Condors generally remain on roosts until much later in morning than do vultures or eagles.

**Voice:** Usually silent but occasionally hisses and grunts.

**Nest:** None constructed. Egg deposited in cliff cavity, cave, pothole, or cave-like hollow in large tree (rarely).

**Egg:** 1, greenish-white to dull white. Very large. Incubation period about 42 days.

**Food:** Carrion (chiefly cattle but sometimes deer and other animals).

**Habitat:** Mostly mountains but occasionally grasslands and other open areas.

**Range:** California; Los Angeles to Santa Clara and Fresno counties, mountains near southern end of San Joaquin Valley, and Sierra Nevada foothills as far north as Fresno County. At least two subpopulations recognized; one living in Coast Range Mountains, the other occupying Transverse Ranges, Tehachapi Mountains, and Sierra Nevadas. Separation zone for two populations near Ventura-Santa Barbara county border. See map 1.

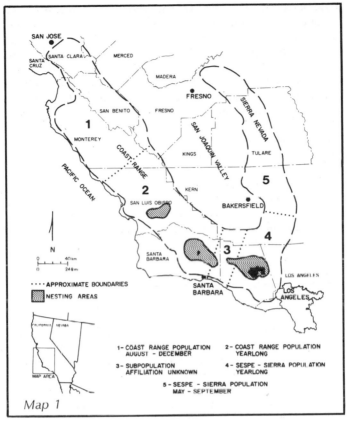

The geographic and seasonal distribution of California Condor subpopulations and current nesting areas (Wilbur, 1978).
Map courtesy of U.S. Fish and Wildlife Service.

# Ospreys: Pandionidae

The single species of Osprey occurs throughout the world. Although it is still common in parts of North America, it has seriously declined in numbers in the East. However, some eastern populations have recently shown improvements in breeding.

### Osprey *Pandion haliaetus*

**Wingspread:** 54 to 72 inches (137 to 182 centimeters).
**Length:** 21 to 24½ inches (53 to 62 centimeters).

**Field Recognition:** Eagle-like hawk generally associated with aquatic ecosystems. *Adult (male)*—Typical example of subspecies *P. h. carolinensis,* of North America, large, dark brown above, and white below. Black patch extends through cheeks and eyes, contrasting with white head. Breast varies from pure white on some birds to slightly streaked with brown on others. Wings frequently deeply bent (crooked); wrist black. Sometimes confused with Bald Eagles, but Ospreys' white underparts separate them. Non-migratory birds of southern Florida (Florida Bay and Everglades National Park) closer in color to *P. h. ridgwayi,* of Bahamas and coastal Yucatán and northern Belize; exhibit exceptional whiteness, often white breasts, sometimes almost completely white heads. Eyes yellow; cere grayish-blue; legs and feet greenish-white. *Adult (female)*—Similar to male but with breast always boldly streaked with brown. *Immature*—Similar to adults, but with white spotting on back. *Chick*—Covered with pale pinkish-buff natal down.

**Flight Style:** Soars on updrafts with wings deeply bent or crooked (an excellent characteristic). Wings appear bowed when seen head-on. When soaring in thermal, however, wings and tail extended or fully spread to achieve maximum lift. Commonly hovers over water when fishing.

**Voice:** Melodious series of *chewk-chewk-chewk* or *tchip-tchip-tchip* whistles uttered while fishing; ringing *kip-kip-kip-kiweeek-kiweeek* alarm note; various other notes.

**Nest:** Large stick structure placed near top of dead or living tree, post, utility pole, duck blind, billboard, roof, tank, channel buoy, or other elevated structure; occasionally on ground. Nests repaired and used year after year.

**Eggs:** 3 (rarely 2 or 4) white to pinkish-cinnamon with numerous reddish-brown blotches. Incubation period 32 to 33 days.

*Osprey nest and eggs.*

*Osprey nest in a dead cedar tree.*

**Food:** Mostly fish; rarely injured birds, frogs, and crustacea.
**Habitat:** Ponds, lakes, rivers, coastal areas. Commonly migrates along coastlines and inland mountains.
**Range:** Nearly cosmopolitan. In Americas from northern Canada and Alaska south (in winter) to Chile, Argentina, Paraguay, and southern Brazil.

# Kites, Hawks, Eagles, Harriers: Accipitridae

Most diurnal birds of prey belong to this large raptor family whose species are diverse in habits and structure. The birds are further divided into several subfamilies.

## White-tailed Kite *Elanus leucurus*

**Wingspread:** 40 inches (101 centimeters).

**Length:** 15 to 17 inches (38 to 43 centimeters).

**Field Recognition:** *Adult (sexes similar)*—Subspecies *E. l. majusculus,* of North America, white with black shoulders and grayish wings on uppersides. Undersides of body and wings white, with dark wrist patch. Wings pointed; whitish tail long. Eyes orange-rufous. Cere buffy. Bill black. Legs and feet buffy yellow. *Immature (sexes similar)*—Head and body streaked with orange-brown; otherwise similar to adult. *Chick*—Covered with dull white to pinkish-buff natal down, followed by second bluish down.

**Flight Style:** Gull-like with tips of wings pointed downward. Frequently hovers.

**Voice:** Chirped or whistled *kewp;* also *eee-grack.*

**Nest:** Stick and twig structure placed in trees and shrubs.

**Eggs:** 4 or 5 (rarely 3 to 6) white to creamy white boldly and extensively blotched with brown. Incubation period about 30 days.

**Food:** Mice, other small mammals, small birds, lizards, and amphibians.

**Habitat:** River valleys, marshes, and foothills which are open.

**Range:** Distributed locally from southern United States (chiefly California where numbers are increasing) south to central Argentina and Chile.

## Swallow-tailed Kite *Elanoides forficatus*

**Wingspread:** 45 to 50 inches (114 to 127 centimeters).

**Length:** 23 to 25 inches (58 to 63 centimeters).

**Field Recognition:** *Adult (sexes similar)*—Head and undersides of body white. Back, flight feathers of wings, and tail dark gray; tail deeply forked. In North American subspecies *E. f. forficatus* upperside of wings has purplish gloss. Eyes reddish-brown; cere bluish; bill black; legs and feet pale bluish-gray. *Immature (sexes similar)*—Similar to adult but back feathers tipped with white; white body narrowly streaked with black. *Chick*—Covered with buffy white natal down, darker on nape and breast.

**Flight Style:** Graceful and buoyant, sometimes in small flocks.

**Voice:** Repetitious, high-pitched *eee* or *kee;* also hissing, high-pitched whistle.
**Nest:** Twig, pine needle, and Spanish moss structure placed at top of tall, slender trees.
**Eggs:** 2 (occasionally 3 or 4) white or creamy, boldly blotched with bright brown. Incubation period 21 to 24 days.
**Food:** Large flying insects, birds (nestlings), snakes, lizards, and occasionally other items.
**Habitat:** Swampy forests, montane pine woods, open marshland.
**Range:** Gulf coast states south to Argentina, Paraguay, and southern Brazil.

## Hook-billed Kite *Chondrohierax uncinatus*

**Wingspread:** 32 inches (81 centimeters).
**Length:** 15 to 17 inches (38 to 43 centimeters).
**Field Recognition:** Small kite with unusually long, strongly hooked bill. Several color phases, sexual differences, and age and individual variations occur. Presumably *C. u. aquilonis* subspecies reaches southwestern United States. *Adult male (normal phase)*—Slaty gray on head and upperparts, lighter gray below; lightly marked with white bars on body but boldly barred with white on undersides of primaries. Tail blackish-gray with two broad, pale gray bars and narrow white tip. *Adult female (normal phase)*—Head gray, body brown above and rufous below with bold whitish bars; undersides of primaries gray or rufous-gray with white bars. Tail bars narrower than in male. *Adult (black phase)*—Completely black (both sexes) with tail marked by one broad white bar. Black phase birds fairly common. All adults (regardless of color phase) have white irises, yellow patch in front of each eye, cere bright pea green, and feet bright yellow to orange. *Immature (normal phase)*—White with black cap and back, tail with gray tip and three or four narrow pale gray and/or white bars. *Immature (black phase)*—Entirely brownish-black. *Chick*—Covered with long white down, washed pinkish on crown, back, and wings.
**Flight Style:** Generally secretive forest bird, soars occasionally on long, elliptical wings. Typical flight alternates flaps with short glides, wings horizontal.
**Voice:** Musical whistle similar to oriole's song; screams and harsh chatters when alarmed; also loud, shrill screams.
**Nest:** Stick and twig structure placed in tree.
**Eggs:** 2, creamy white blotched with chocolate brown. Incubation period unknown.
**Food:** Chiefly land snails; rarely frogs, salamanders, and insects.
**Habitat:** Lower forest canopy, dense undergrowth in swampy areas, occasional dry tropical forest and even temperate areas up to elevations of 6,000 feet or more.

**Range:** Recently extreme southern Texas (Santa Ana National Wildlife Refuge) south to northern Argentina, Paraguay, eastern Peru, and Bolivia; Trinidad; Lesser Antilles; Grenada; and Cuba.

## Mississippi Kite *Ictinia mississippiensis*

**Wingspread:** 34 to 37 inches (86 to 94 centimeters).
**Length:** 13 to 17 inches (33 to 43 centimeters).
**Field Recognition:** Falcon-like with long, pointed wings. Females average considerably larger than males. *Adult*—Head pale gray, somewhat darker in female. Back and uppersides of wings dark gray. Underparts paler gray; tail completely black. *Immature*—Head pale with dark streaks. Undersides of body heavily streaked with brown. Tail dark with three or four lighter bars and lighter tip. Eyes deep red, somewhat lighter in immatures. *Chick*—Covered with white natal down tinged with buff on upperparts.
**Flight Style:** Graceful, smooth, and buoyant; sometimes slow with much easy flapping. Resembles medium-size gull at times. Frequently seen in flocks which during migration can become large (200 or more birds).
**Voice:** *Phee-phew; kee-ee.*
**Nest:** Twig structure, or old crow's nest, lined with green leaves or twigs, placed from 10 feet (3 meters) above ground to crotch or fork high in tall tree.
**Eggs:** 2 (sometimes 1 or 3) white to pale bluish-white. Incubation period 30 to 32 days.

B.M.S.

*Mississippi Kite nest and eggs.*

**Food:** Mainly insects; rarely birds, bats, lizards, frogs, and fish.
**Habitat:** Wooded creek bottoms, wooded areas adjacent to farmland, and open shrubland.
**Range:** Nests locally in southern and south central United States (Kansas, Iowa, Tennessee, and South Carolina southward to northwestern Florida, Gulf coast west to Arizona). Migrates through Central America; some winter as far south as Paraguay and Argentina. Winter range poorly known because of confusion in distinguishing this species from very similar Plumbeous Kite (*I. plumbea*) of Central and South America.

## Snail (Everglade) Kite *Rostrhamus sociabilis*

**Wingspread:** 44 to 45 inches (111 to 114 centimeters).
**Length:** 16 to 18 inches (40 to 45 centimeters).
**Field Recognition:** Medium-size kite with proportionately broader wings than other North American kites; bill very slender and strongly hooked. Florida subspecies *R. s. plumbeus* endangered. *Adult (male)*—Slaty black with white upper and lower tail coverts, white rump, square or slightly forked black tail with narrow white tip and broad white basal area. Eyelids and area in front of eyes flame scarlet; iris carmine; bill black; legs apricot-orange. *Adult (female)*—Brown above with white forehead and throat; sometimes whitish line behind eye. Dusky brown below, heavily blotched with rufous or white circular marks; rump white; tail brown with narrow white tip and broad white basal area. *Sub-adult (male)*—Similar to adult male but upperparts tinged with fuscous. Broad cinnamon-buff streaking on chin, throat, breast, and middle abdomen. Breast streaks dark rufous shading to deep chestnut. *Sub-adult (female)*—Similar to adult female but with white and black streaks on top of head and nape; whitish to pinkish-buff underparts heavily streaked with fuscous-black. Thighs also cinnamon-buff, as are underwing coverts, also having brownish-black streaks. *Immature (sexes similar)*—Similar to sub-adult female but more richly colored and darker. Chestnut brown streaked with darker brown, yellow, and white; throat and conspicuous line behind eye white; tail as in adults. Upper tail coverts light buffy; tail brownish-black on upperside with broad cinnamon-buff tip. Immature (juvenile) retains plumage through first winter during which time plumage fades, assuming sub-adult plumage following summer or autumn. *Chick*—Covered with buffy natal down tinged with cinnamon on crown, wings, and rump; second down thicker and darker grayish-brown.
**Flight Style:** "Floppy," suggesting heron's wingbeat; less graceful than most other kites. When hunting snails kites fly slowly over marsh at low altitude, moving back and forth searching for prey. When snail is seen kite drops swiftly and clutches prey

with talons, then carries snail to well-used feeding perch where it is extracted and swallowed whole.

**Voice:** Cackling *kor-ee-ee-a kor-ee-ee-a* cry.

**Nest:** Bulky, somewhat flattened stick platform, lined with leaves, vines, and Spanish moss, placed from 3 to 15 feet (0.9 to 4.5 meters) above water in shrubs, trees, or saw grass.

**Eggs:** 3 or 4 (occasionally 2, rarely up to 6) white extensively blotched with brown. Incubation period unknown.

**Food:** Almost entirely freshwater snails of genus *Pomacea* (in Florida *P. paludosa*); rarely mites, midge larva, and plant debris. All may have been eaten accidentally while swallowing snails.

**Habitat:** Freshwater marshes, open swamps, large lakes and rivers where *Pomacea* snails occur.

**Range:** Southern Florida in marshes along southwestern and western shoreline of Lake Okeechobee; southwestern corner of Loxahatchee National Wildlife Refuge and eastern portion of pool 2A in Conservation Area 2; eastern Mexico south to pampas of Argentina and Uruguay; Cuba and Isle of Pines. See map 2.

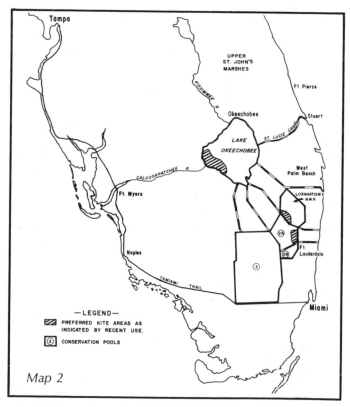

The geographic range of the Snail Kite in southern Florida.
Map courtesy of U.S. Fish and Wildlife Service.

# Northern Goshawk *Accipiter gentilis*

**Wingspread:** 40 to 47 inches (101 to 119 centimeters).
**Length:** 20 to 26½ inches (51 to 67 centimeters).
**Field Recognition:** *Adult*—Subspecies *A. g. atricapillus,* distributed widely in North America, dark bluish-gray or grayish on upperparts and pale grayish-white on undersides marked with fine dark bars. Dark cap and cheek, bold white eyebrow line are distinctive. Adults and immatures sometimes show conspicuous white undertail coverts. Wings proportionally longer and broader than other accipiters. Tail long, tip slightly to moderately rounded. Iris red to orange; cere and legs yellow. Subspecies *A. g. laingi,* on islands off British Columbia coast, similar to previous subspecies but slightly darker, particularly in immature plumage; subspecies *A. g. apache,* of southern Arizona and New Mexico mountains (and northwestern Mexico), differs from *atricapillus* only by being somewhat larger and with heavier feet. *Immature*—Brown on upperparts, usually with bold white eyebrow line; whitish on undersides with heavy brown streaking formed by bold, dark brown drop-shaped marks. White undertail coverts also have bold, dark brown drop-shaped marks lacking in other accipiters. If bird is seen perched at close range this feature may help distinguish immature Northern Goshawk from immature Cooper's Hawk; probably not helpful for birds in flight. *Chick*—Covered with short white natal down, later changing to longer woolly down tinged with gray on back.
**Flight Style:** Generally several heavy flapping wingbeats, then brief period of sailing, followed by more wingbeats. Heavier and more direct flight than exhibited by smaller accipiters. Rarely soars; at times flight deceptively similar to that of Gyrfalcon.
**Voice:** *Ca-ca-ca-ca* or *kuk-kuk-kuk* screamed in alarm; occasionally other calls used at nest.
**Nest:** Large, flat, stick platform, sometimes used for several years in succession, placed in crotch of tall tree or on limb from 30 to 60 feet (9 to 18 meters) above ground.
**Eggs:** 3 (rarely 1 to 5) dirty white or pale bluish. Incubation period about 36 to 38 days.
**Food:** Large and medium-size mammals and birds. In New York and Pennsylvania, Red Squirrels and American Crows important food items; other species taken in much smaller numbers.
**Habitat:** Forests and extensive woodlands. Coastlines, mountain ridges, and Great Lakes shorelines during migration.
**Range:** Holarctic; from treeline south to southern Appalachians in East, and Mexico in West.

## Sharp-shinned Hawk *Accipiter striatus*

**Wingspread:** 20 to 27 inches (50 to 68 centimeters).
**Length:** 10 to 14 inches (25 to 35 centimeters).
**Field Recognition:** Smallest North American accipiter. Eyes proportionally larger than in other North American accipiters, giving somewhat "pop-eyed" appearance when seen at close range; feature can sometimes help in distinguishing immature Sharpshins from immature Cooper's Hawks if used in combination with other field marks. *Adult*—Widespread continental subspecies *A. s. velox* bluish-gray on upperparts and whitish with reddish-brown bars on underside. Wings short and rounded; long tail has three gray bars and narrow white tip which can be notched, square, or occasionally slightly rounded. Subspecies *A. s. perobscurus,* of Queen Charlotte Islands, British Columbia, slightly darker than *velox.* However, *A. s. suttoni,* of forested mountains of southern Arizona, New Mexico, and portions of Mexico strikingly different from *velox:* paler below with attractive wash of rufous on undersides and unbarred rufous thighs. Eye red (variable in some subspecies); legs and feet yellow. *Immature*—Brown above, white below, with bold brown streaks formed by small drop-shaped brown spots. Streaks generally cover most of underside, whereas in many (but not all) immature Cooper's Hawks streaking covers only anterior half or three-quarters of underside. Suggestion of pale eyebrow line seen on some birds; this is not useful field mark and should not be confused with similar mark on Cooper's Hawks and especially on Northern Goshawk. As birds begin to acquire adult plumage some barring and streaking appear on breast. Eye yellow; legs and feet yellowish. *Chick*—Covered with creamy white or yellowish down followed by second longer white down with some grayish on back. *Identification Note:* Field marks published to aid in flight identification of some Sharp-shinned Hawks (large females) and some Cooper's Hawks (small males) based upon relative extent to which head of bird protrudes from, or is tucked into, shoulders (Brett and Nagy, *Feathers in the Wind,* 1973). Head tucked deeply into shoulders, bird is considered Sharpshin; head protrudes extensively from shoulders, considered Cooper's Hawk. However, degree to which hawk's head is tucked into, or protrudes from, shoulders varies considerably depending upon size of bird, flight style, positions of wings at any particular moment, and wind conditions. While field mark generally applies to some Sharp-shinned Hawks (birds with tips of tails notched or square), mark does not seem to apply consistently to many large female Sharp-shins or to some Cooper's Hawks. Therefore, use head-to-shoulder profile cautiously, in combination with other field marks discussed under appropriate species accounts, to arrive at identification of accipiters. Impossi-

ble to identify some birds correctly; when in doubt never hesitate to list bird as unidentified. Cooper's Hawks less common than Sharp-shinned Hawks, especially in East.

**Flight Style:** Several rapid wingbeats, then brief period of sailing, followed by more wingbeats. Soars in thermals occasionally with wings and tail fully spread. In general, lighter and more buoyant flight than exhibited by other accipiters.

**Voice:** Thin, repeated *kik-kik-kik* cackle higher in pitch than in larger accipiters.

**Nest:** Large twig platform, generally on branch or in crotch of conifer but occasionally in oak tree, lined with twigs, strips, or chips of bark.

**Eggs:** 4 or 5 (occasionally 3, rarely 6 to 8) white or bluish-white with brown and/or purple marks. Incubation period 34 to 35 days.

**Food:** Mostly small birds, but occasionally small mammals, lizards, and insects.

**Habitat:** Normally forests and woodlands, but during migration coastlines, mountains, and Great Lakes shorelines.

**Range:** Treeline of North America south to Argentina, Paraguay, Uruguay, and southern Brazil; West Indies.


## Cooper's Hawk *Accipiter cooperii*

**Wingspread:** 27 to 36 inches (68 to 91 centimeters).
**Length:** 14 to 20 inches (35 to 50 centimeters).
**Field Recognition:** Most difficult of accipiters to identify. Intermediate in size between Sharp-shinned Hawk and Northern Goshawk. Essentially larger version of Sharp-shin but with tail somewhat longer in proportion to rest of body as compared with Sharp-shinned Hawk; tip of tail usually well rounded. Some large immature Cooper's Hawks similar in appearance to small immature Northern Goshawks, but Cooper's Hawk tail usually more rounded with undertail coverts unmarked. Northern Goshawk has more heft, heavier wingbeats, broader wings, and shorter tail. In addition, some Cooper's Hawks have narrow white eyebrow line similar to some immature Northern Goshawks' line but much less conspicuous. Nevertheless observers should be cautious about not confusing this line with that of Northern Goshawks. *Adult (male)*—Bluish-gray on upperparts (darkest on back) with black cap; whitish below richly marked with reddish-brown bars, tending to give birds richer appearance than generally smaller Sharp-shinned Hawk. Tail bluish-gray with three black bands and narrow, white, well-rounded tip. Eye red; cere yellow; legs and feet deep yellow. *Adult (female)*—Similar to adult male but back browner rather than bluish-gray. Considerably larger than male, sometimes almost size of small

Northern Goshawks. *Immature*—Brown above, white below marked with fine to broad dark brown streaks, *or* with bold, dark brown club-shaped spots making it necessary to avoid mistaking these birds for immature Northern Goshawks. Streaks or spots usually cover upper half or three-quarters of underside of body; occasionally bird has most of underside well marked. Immature plumage larger and less compact than adult plumage, giving young birds larger appearance. Eye yellow; legs and feet yellow. *Chick*—Covered with short, creamy-white natal down soon replaced with short silky-white down.

**Flight Style:** Similar to Sharp-shinned Hawk but wingbeats sufficiently slower to enable experienced observers to recognize differences in many instances. Generally more direct flight than that of Sharp-shinned Hawk, also soaring more than Sharp-shin.

**Voice:** Harsh, staccato *ca-ca-ca-ca* cackling; dozens of additional calls used in specific situations.

**Nest:** Large twig platform, lined with hemlock, oak, or maple bark, placed in crotch of tree or on limb next to trunk.

**Eggs:** 4 or 5 (rarely 3 to 6) pale sky blue fading to dirty white, occasionally spotted lightly. Incubation period 35 to 36 days.

**Food:** Medium-size birds (particularly starlings, flickers, and meadowlarks), small mammals (including Red Squirrels and chipmunks), lizards, amphibians, and large insects.

**Habitat:** Mature forested and wooded areas, large woodlots, riverine woodland, and canyons. During migration, along coastlines, mountain ridges, and Great Lakes shorelines.

**Range:** Southern Canada south to Gulf coast and northwestern Mexico. Migrants occasionally reach extreme northern South America.


# Red-tailed Hawk *Buteo jamaicensis*

**Wingspread:** 46 to 58 inches (116 to 147 centimeters).
**Length:** 19 to 25½ inches (48 to 64 centimeters).
**Field Recognition:** Soaring hawk with broad wings and tail. Extremely variable in color. *Adult*—Typical individual of eastern subspecies *B. j. borealis,* which ranges westward to Great Plains, brown above and white below with vivid reddish-chestnut tail (lighter on underside) and conspicuous belly band of dark streaks. In some birds belly band very faint or lacking entirely. Seen head-on, light cere at base of bill and light wrist area on leading edge of each wing frequently produce "headlights," visible at great distance in some birds. Western subspecies differ considerably from eastern race. *B. j. calurus,* of much of West, often resembles *borealis* but has narrow black subterminal band on tail; most individuals, even very dark or black ones, recognized by darker belly and upper breast, enclosing paler area on mid-breast. *B. j. harlani,* breeding in Alberta, British Columbia,

and parts of Alaska, occurs in dark (often black) color phase with body black or dark sooty, wing lining black flecked with white, wingtips black, primaries and secondaries light on underside, and tail grayish with dusky (not red) mottling, blending into broad, dark subterminal band. Rarer light (sometimes almost white) color phase also occurs in. which body is white with narrow, dark belly band and tail similar to that of dark phase birds; some *harlani* show mixture of characteristics of both color phases. *B. j. alascensis,* of southeastern Alaska south to Queen Charlotte Islands, resembles eastern *borealis,* but is smaller. *B. j. kriderii,* of Great Plains, pale with tail almost white. *B. j. fuertesi,* of southern Texas, New Mexico, and parts of adjacent Mexico, pale and white below with almost no belly band. *B. j. umbrinus,* of Florida peninsula and Bahamas, similar to eastern *borealis* but has dark bars near shafts of rectrices and is smaller. *Immature*— Similar to adult, but tail grayish-brown (in typical eastern bird) with narrow blackish bars instead of rich reddish-chestnut as in adult. Enormous variation in western birds. *Chick*—Covered with grayish or buffy-white natal down, later changing to woolly white down.

**Flight Style:** Frequently soars on partly folded wings on updrafts along mountains and bluffs; wingbeats used occasionally. Tail not spread. At other times soars in thermals in wide circles with wings and tail spread completely. While hunting, may hover briefly or hang motionless in mid-air.

**Voice:** Hoarse, rasping *tsee-eeee-arrr* scream lasting 2 or 3 seconds.

**Nest:** Large twig and stick platform, lined with bark, cornstalks, and similar material, placed in trees, cacti, towers, ledges, rock pinnacles, and similar places.

**Eggs:** 2 or 3 (rarely 1 or 4) whitish to bluish-white blotched with brown. Incubation period 28 to 32 days, typically 30 days.

**Food:** Varied; rodents, rabbits, snakes (including rattlesnakes), lizards, birds (especially pheasants), and occasionally other items.

**Habitat:** Mountains, woodland, deserts, fields, agricultural areas, and other open country.

**Range:** Treeline of North America south to western Panama; West Indies.


# Red-shouldered Hawk *Buteo lineatus*

**Wingspread:** 32 to 50 inches (81 to 127 centimeters).
**Length:** 17 to 24 inches (43 to 61 centimeters).
**Field Recognition:** Moderate-size soaring hawk with richly colored plumage. *Adult (both sexes)*—Most widely distributed eastern subspecies *B. l. lineatus* blackish-brown on upperparts with reddish shoulder patches on uppersides of wings, crescent-shaped "windows" (areas of translucence) in primaries when

seen in flight, richly colored reddish underparts, and vividly banded black and white tail. *B. l. alleni,* of Florida (except extreme southern part) and westward along Gulf coast to eastern Texas, somewhat smaller and paler than *lineatus. B. l. extimus,* of extreme southern Florida and Keys, even smaller than *alleni* and paler to field observers than *lineatus. B. l. texanus,* of south-central Texas coast south to Mexico City, somewhat smaller than eastern *lineatus* and more rufous. Isolated lowland riverine valley subspecies *B. l. elegans,* of southern Oregon south to northern Baja California, even more rufous than *texanus* on undersides but less rufous on back. *Immature (both sexes)*—Brown above with white eyebrow line similar to that of immature Northern Goshawk (with which these birds are sometimes confused), white on underparts with heavy brown streaks, tinge of rufous on shoulders, and "windows" on wings when seen in flight. *Chick*—Covered with buffy-white natal down.

**Flight Style:** Rapid wingbeats often followed by brief sail. More or less suggests accipiter's flight. Occasionally soars in thermals.

**Voice:** Distinctive *kee-aah* or *kee-oow* scream, with second syllable more prolonged and lower in pitch than first.

**Nest:** Twig and stick platform placed in large tree (or palmetto in Florida); occasionally abandoned hawk, crow, or squirrel nest is used.

**Eggs:** 3 (sometimes 2 to 5) whitish blotched with brown, chestnut, and lilac. Incubation period about 28 days.

**Food:** Varied; small mammals, snakes, lizards, turtles, frogs, toads, small birds, grasshoppers, crayfish, occasional other items.

**Habitat:** Broken wet forested or wooded areas and lowland riverine valleys.

**Range:** Southern Canada south to Florida Keys, Gulf coast south to central Mexico, and isolated population from southern Oregon south to Baja California.

## Broad-winged Hawk *Buteo platypterus*

**Wingspread:** 32 to 39 inches (81 to 99 centimeters).
**Length:** 13½ to 19 inches (34 to 48 centimeters).
**Field Recognition:** Chunky, crow-size eastern soaring hawk represented by subspecies *B. p. platypterus* in North America. *Adult (normal phase)*—Brown on upperparts, throat white, chest chestnut, underparts white barred with brown. Tail distinctive with two white and two black bands. Large light area (cere and small portion of forehead) behind bill suggests "headlight" when hawk is seen head-on. Wings sometimes held in slightly bowed position when bird soars or glides on updrafts along mountains. Eye light reddish-hazel; bill bluish-black; cere yellow; legs and feet yellow. *Adult (dark phase)*—Completely sooty brown. Extremely rare. Individuals observed migrating southward past Pt. Diablo

near San Francisco, California, and in Midwest. *Immature*—
Brown above, white below with brown streaks. Tail has narrow
gray bands. *Chick*—Covered with short dusky-white natal down.
**Flight Style:** Frequently forms large flocks or "kettles" in thermals during migration, then glides to new thermals and repeats
process. Western Swainson's Hawk also uses this technique;
sometimes both species form mixed flocks in Southwest and
Central America. During breeding season individual birds sometimes seen soaring in wide circles over eastern forests and
wooded areas.
**Voice:** Shrill, high-pitched *pweeeeee* or *ker-wee-eeee* whistle.
**Nest:** Twig and stick platform, sometimes repaired hawk, crow,
or squirrel nest, placed in trees at heights ranging from 3 to 90
feet (0.9 to 27 meters) above ground. Oak and pine chips, green
sprigs, line nest.

*Broad-winged Hawk nest and eggs.*

**Eggs:** 2 or 3 (rarely 1 or 4) dull creamy white blotched with
brown. Incubation period about 30 days.
**Food:** Small mammals, snakes, toads, frogs, large insects, occasionally small birds, and other items.
**Habitat:** Deciduous forests and woodlands. Also mixed forests.
**Range:** Deciduous and mixed forests from Alberta eastward to
Nova Scotia and southward to Florida and Texas. Some birds
stray westward to Great Plains and migrants pass through southeastern Texas, rarely down Pacific coast.

## Short-tailed Hawk *Buteo brachyurus*

**Wingspread:** 35 inches (89 centimeters).
**Length:** 14 to 17 inches (35 to 43 centimeters).
**Field Recognition:** Small (crow-size) hawk of Central and South America barely reaching North America. Few hundred individuals of subspecies *B. b. fuliginosus* occur in Florida. *Adult (normal phase)*—Head, back, and primaries dark, contrasting with otherwise white throat and body; small whitish area on lower forehead behind bill. Tail grayish-brown with narrow white tip, broader black band behind tip, and three or four additional narrow black bands (broken or reduced in older birds). Bill black; eyes brown; cere, legs, and feet yellow. *Adult (black phase)*—Entirely sooty black to chocolate brown with small whitish area on lower forehead and conspicuous white area on underside of each wing. *Immature (normal phase)*—Buffy and similar to immature Broad-winged Hawk. *Immature (black phase)*—Similar to black phase adult but with more bands on tail. Partly concealed white or buffy body feathers sometimes make undersides appear spotted. *Chick*—Covered with creamy-white natal down.
**Flight Style:** Soars on motionless wings. When hunting sometimes hangs motionless in mid-air, then stoops.
**Voice:** High-pitched scream intermediate between that of Red-shouldered Hawk and Broad-winged Hawk.
**Nest:** Large stick and twig structure, lined with green leaves, placed from 8 to 90 feet (2.4 to 27 meters) above ground in cypress, gum, or magnolia trees, mangroves, or cabbage palms.
**Eggs:** 2 (sometimes 1 or 3) pale bluish-white often blotched with brown. Incubation period unknown.
**Food:** Rodents, birds, lizards, and insects.
**Habitat:** Generally cypress and mangrove swamps, occasionally pine areas and open terrain.
**Range:** Central Mexico south to Chile, Peru, Argentina, Paraguay, Bolivia, and Brazil. In addition to small Florida population there are few hypothetical Texas records. Florida birds occur in central and southern part of state (rarely in northern Florida) from late February through early October. From mid-October through early February population apparently migrates southward to extreme southern part of Florida mainland, with substantial numbers wintering within and close to Everglade National Park. Population within state numbers about 200 birds.

## Swainson's Hawk *Buteo swainsoni*

**Wingspread:** 47 to 57 inches (119 to 144 centimeters).
**Length:** 19 to 22 inches (48 to 55 centimeters).
**Field Recognition:** Common soaring hawk of Great Plains and West. Occurs in light, dark, and rufous color phases; light phase

birds are most common. *Adult (light phase)*—Head, back, chest, and primaries dark brown, contrasting with otherwise white underparts. Tail light with numerous narrow, dark bands and wider, dark subterminal band. Eye brown; bill blackish; cere pale greenish-yellow; legs and feet light yellow. *Adult (dark phase)*—Rare; entirely blackish except for light throat, forehead, undertail coverts, and cloudy or dark buffy wing linings. *Adult (rufous phase)*—Somewhat like dark phase but lighter brown on underparts with rusty brown blotches and bars. Intermediate color forms between all color phases. *Immature*—Dark brown above, light rufous below with brown chest and much brown streaking. Birds also have whitish eyebrow line. *Chick*—Covered with white natal down.

**Flight Style:** Forms large flocks or kettles during migration. Soars with wings held in slight V or dihedral.

**Voice:** Long, shrill *kreeeeeer* whistle.

**Nest:** Large twig, grass, and weed structure lined with bark, green leaves, down, and other materials, placed in giant cactus, low tree, cliff, rocky pinnacle, or on ground.

**Eggs:** 2 (rarely 3 or 4) white with pale brown markings. Incubation period about 28 days.

**Food:** Insects (especially orthoptera), rodents, bats, reptiles, amphibians, and some birds (injured or young).

**Habitat:** Mixed deciduous-coniferous parklands, rangeland and foothills, plains. During migration hawks sometimes occur over high meadows and mountain ridges in Rockies.

**Range:** Great Plains and West from interior Alaska south to northern Mexico. Winters mostly on Argentine pampas; in recent years a few immature Swainson's Hawks have wintered in southern Florida. Rarely seen in East although few individuals observed during spring and autumn in recent years.

## Zone-tailed Hawk *Buteo albonotatus*

**Wingspread:** 47 to 53 inches (119 to 134 centimeters).

**Length:** 18½ to 21½ inches (47 to 54 centimeters).

**Field Recognition:** Slender, grayish-black hawk of Southwest. *Adult (sexes similar)*—Grayish-black with undersides of wings two-toned (similar to Turkey Vulture); dark tail offset by three bands and narrow white tip. Small whitish area on forehead behind cere. Eyes reddish-brown; bill horn at base and black at tip; cere, mouth corners, legs, and feet yellow. *Immature*—Similar to adult but somewhat browner with white spots scattered on underside; tail marked with numerous bands. *Chick*—Covered with grayish natal down.

**Flight Style:** Similar to Turkey Vulture (with which often compared) but sluggish compared with vultures. Sometimes soars like buteo on flat wings and with tail spread.

**Voice:** Feeble squealing whistle similar to Red-tailed Hawk's.

**Nest:** Bulky stick platform with green leaves placed 25 to 100 feet (7.5 to 30 meters) above ground in pine, cottonwood, or mesquite (rarely).

**Eggs:** 2 (rarely 1 or 3) bluish-white or white occasionally slightly spotted. Incubation period unknown.

**Food:** Lizards, frogs, small fish, and sometimes small mammals and birds.

**Habitat:** Desert mountains, dry country, also rivers and creeks draining from mountainous areas.

**Range:** Southwestern border of United States on middle slopes of mountains in Arizona, New Mexico, and Texas; southward locally to Peru, Paraguay, Bolivia, and Brazil; also Trinidad.

## White-tailed Hawk *Buteo albicaudatus*

**Wingspread:** 48 to 54 inches (122 to 137 centimeters).

**Length:** 23 to 24 inches (54 to 61 centimeters).

**Field Recognition:** Large, stocky, tropical and subtropical hawk represented in North America by subspecies *B. a. hypospodius*. *Adult (male)*—Slaty gray above, undersides and rump white, wings slaty gray with rufous shoulders and white underwing linings; dark wingtips, tail white with blackish subterminal band and very narrow white tip. Eyes brown; cere pale green; bill black; legs and feet yellow. *Adult (female)*—Somewhat darker than male with more rufous on wings. *Immature*—Brownish-black, somewhat lighter on undersides of primaries. *Chick*—Covered with buffy natal down washed with smoky brown on head and wings; blackish around each eye. Appearance distinctively different from chicks of other hawks.

**Flight Style:** Soars high overhead or, at other times, low over ground; also hovers while hunting.

**Voice:** High-pitched, tinkling, *ke-ke-ke-ke* cackle.

**Nest:** Large twig nest mixed with dry grass, lined with green mesquite sprigs or similar material, placed 5 to 15 feet (1.5 to 4.5 meters) above ground in small trees or bushes.

**Eggs:** 2 (sometimes 1 or 3) white sometimes spotted with lavender or brown. Incubation period unknown.

**Food:** Rabbits, rodents, birds (rarely), snakes, lizards, frogs, various insects, and occasionally carrion.

**Habitat:** Coastal prairie (in Texas), chaparral, and open grassy range.

**Range:** From southern Texas south to central Argentina; also Trinidad, the Margarita Islands, Curaçao, Bonaire, and Aruba.

## Rough-legged Hawk *Buteo lagopus*

**Wingspread:** 48 to 56 inches (122 to 142 centimeters).
**Length:** 19 to 24 inches (48 to 61 centimeters).
**Field Recognition:** North American subspecies *B. l. sanctijohannis* extremely variable in color, forming gradation between light colored birds and completely melanistic individuals (see *Condor*, 1955, 57:313–46). For field-identification purposes, however, light and dark color phases recognized. Sex of some adults recognized by differences in pattern of bands on tail. Likewise, juveniles distinguished from adults by pattern of band on tail; sex apparently impossible to determine. See illustration. Wings

R.A.

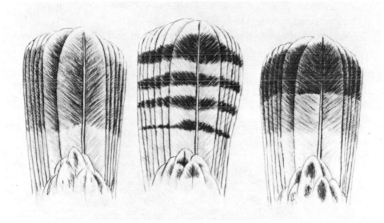

*Tail patterns of Rough-legged Hawks. Juvenile (left), adult male (center), and adult female (right). Little variation occurs in the juvenal plumage, but there is much variation in the tail patterns of adult males and females.*

and tail on all individuals slightly longer than on other buteos. *Adult (light phase)*—Tawny on head and chest with considerable variation in amount of black on belly. Black wrist patch on upper and underside of each wing; generally trailing edge of wings' underside boldly lined with black. Broad black band, separated into lighter and darker segments, near tip of white tail in females; band variable in extent and pattern. Males tend to have broad and 2 to 4 clear-cut but narrower black bands near tip of white tail. Tail band pattern also variable. Legs feathered to toes (in birds of all ages and color phases). Eyes brown to yellow. Cere yellow. Bill dark horn. Legs and feet yellow. *Adult (dark phase*)—Black with much white on undersides of wings. Intermediates also occur between these two color phases. *Immature*—Similar to adults but generally paler on upperside and underside. Sometimes underside snow-white except for black or dark belly band (which can cover entire belly), black wrist patch on underside of each wing, and black wingtips. In some immatures black trailing edge of underside of wings much less prominent or extensive than in adults, or lacking almost entirely. Broad, dark subterminal tail band also less defined than in adult males, but suggests tail band pattern of some adult females unless seen clearly. *Chick*—Covered with pale grayish-brown natal down later replaced with darker, thicker gray down.

**Flight Style:** Soars on updrafts with some flapping and more wrist action than in other buteos. Frequently hovers when hunting.

**Voice:** Loud *kle-kle-kle-kle-ree-hee* screech.

**Nest:** Stick nest lined with green vegetation and placed on rocky ledge or available tree.

**Eggs:** 3 or 4 (sometimes 2 to 7) white blotched with brown. Incubation 28 to 31 days.

F.T.

*Rough-legged Hawk nest and nestlings.*

**Food:** Small mammals (especially lemmings on Arctic nesting grounds) and small birds. *Microtus* voles replace lemmings in hawk's diet on winter range.

**Habitat:** Arctic tundra and coastlines in summer. Marshes, open fields, and prairies in winter.

**Range:** Holarctic; breeds between latitudes 61 degrees and 76 degrees North, and winters southward to central United States (for subspecies *B. l. sanctijohannis*).


# Ferruginous Hawk *Buteo regalis*

**Wingspread:** 56 inches (142 centimeters).

**Length:** 22½ to 25 inches (57 to 63 centimeters).

**Field Recognition:** Large soaring hawk generally standing on ground rather than elevated perches. Three color phases. *Adult (normal phase)*—Brown above streaked with white, and rufous on back and shoulders. White below with some narrow dark streaks on chest and belly. Rufous thighs, marked with black bars, form conspicuous V on underside when bird observed overhead in flight. Tail whitish washed with ash. Legs feathered to toes (in all ages and color phases). Eyes pale yellow; cere and gape bright yellow; bill dark horn; legs and feet yellow. *Adult (black phase)*—Entirely dark brown except for wings and tail which resemble birds in normal color phase. *Adult (red phase)*—Essentially more rufous version of black color phase. *Immature*—Dark brown on upperparts and white below (including thighs) with some darker flecks. Rump white. Tail grayish, occasionally with several faint dusky bars. *Chick*—Covered with white natal down, washed with gray on crown and back. Later thicker white down develops.

**Flight Style:** Takes off with heavy, sluggish wingbeats but soars well when aloft. Sometimes zigzags low over ground similar to Northern Harrier. Occasionally hovers.

**Voice:** Loud *kree-a* or harshly uttered gull-like *kaah kaah*.

**Nest:** Stick structure lined with sagebrush roots, bones, horse or cow dung, placed amid hillside boulders, in bush, or in tree.

**Eggs:** 3 or 4 (occasionally 5) bluish-white blotched with brown. Incubation period about 28 days.

**Food:** Ground squirrels, prairie dogs, rabbits, mice, birds (occasionally), snakes, and insects.

**Habitat:** Open prairie and (in winter) mixed pineries and grassy glades.

**Range:** Breeds from eastern Washington and southern Alberta, Saskatchewan, and Manitoba southward to eastern Oregon, Nevada, New Mexico, Texas, and Oklahoma. Winters from southwestern United States southward to northern Mexico (including Baja California).

## Gray Hawk *Buteo nitidus*

**Wingspread:** 32 to 38 inches (81 to 96 centimeters).
**Length:** 16 to 18 inches (40 to 45 centimeters).
**Field Recognition:** Small tropical and subtropical soaring hawk represented in North America by subspecies *B. n. plagiatus.* *Adult (male)*—Ashy gray above, whitish below with dark gray barrings. Tail coverts white, tail black with white tip and two or three bold white bands suggesting that of Broad-winged Hawk. Eyes dark brown; cere yellow; bill bluish-black; legs and feet yellow. *Adult (female)*—Darker gray above than in adult male; coarser barring on undersides. *Immature*—Dark brown above, buffy below with dark brown streaks. Rump white. Tail has numerous dark bands with narrow white tip; longer than in adult birds. Cere and legs also less vivid than in adults. *Chick*—Covered with white natal down with gray tinge on back.
**Flight Style:** Powerful and swift, falcon-like, but more soaring than falcons.
**Voice:** Loud, high-pitched *cree-ee-ee* or *cree-eer* somewhat similar to that of Broad-winged Hawk.
**Nest:** Crow-nest-size twig or stick structure, lined with green vegetation, placed high in tree or mesquites but hidden by leaves.
**Eggs:** 2 (occasionally 1 or 3) white or pale blue, generally unmarked, but sometimes slightly spotted. Incubation period unknown.
**Food:** Mostly lizards and small snakes but sometimes rodents and birds.
**Habitat:** Riverine forests and groves in semi-arid regions.
**Range:** Arizona to Texas and southward to Bolivia, Argentina, Paraguay, and Brazil.

## Harris' Hawk *Parabuteo unicinctus*

**Wingspread:** 45 inches (114 centimeters).
**Length:** 17½ to 24 inches (44 to 61 centimeters).
**Field Recognition:** Unusually tame hawk of Southwest sometimes perched in pairs on cactus, tree, or other object. *Adult (sexes similar)*—Typical individual of subspecies *P. u. harrisi,* of southern Texas southward, sooty with chestnut shoulders, thighs, and underwing coverts. Rump and undertail coverts white. Tail sooty with tip and basal half-white. *P. u. superior,* of southeastern California and southwestern Arizona, slightly larger and darker than *harrisi.* Tends to perch conspicuously. Eyes brown; bill gray with black tip; cere, legs, and feet yellow. *Immature (sexes similar)*—Brownish above, light below with buffy streakings, and tail banded. *Chick*—Covered with buffy natal down which changes in about a week to rich brown roughly color of adult's shoulder. Some authors state that dark plumage fades to

pure white rapidly.

**Flight Style:** Generally rapid, direct flight when disturbed. Occasionally soars in wide circles high overhead.

**Voice:** Loud *iirr* when alarmed; several other calls given during nesting cycle.

**Nest:** Stick structure, lined with fresh sprigs of vegetation, placed in tree, high shrub, or Saguaro cactus.

**Eggs:** 3 or 4 (sometimes 1 to 5) unmarked white. Sometimes second clutch deposited in same nest or one nearby after first nesting effort of season completed. Incubation period 33 to 36 days, generally about 35 days.

**Food:** Rabbits, small mammals, birds, and lizards. Apparently snakes not taken, or rarely even when abundant.

**Habitat:** Chaparral, riverine wooded areas, and savannah country.

**Range:** In United States confined to Mexican border from Arizona to Texas. Ranges south to Chile, Argentina, Paraguay, and eastward to Brazil and Venezuela.

## Common Black Hawk *Buteogallus anthracinus*

**Wingspread:** 48 inches (122 centimeters).

**Length:** 20 to 23 inches (50 to 58 centimeters).

**Field Recognition:** Subspecies *B. a. anthracinus* occurs in North America. *Adult (sexes similar)*—Sooty black (tinged with brown in worn plumage), tail with broad white band in middle and white tip. In flight wings unusually wide with light base of primaries area on underside of each wing somewhat similar to that of Black Vulture. Eyes brown. Bill mostly black with white tip. Cere, legs, and feet yellow. *Immature (sexes similar)*—Brownish-black above with streaks of rufous, buffy, and white. Underparts whitish to buffy-orange; strongly streaked with black on breast. *Chick*—Covered with white natal down on head and breast, grayish elsewhere.

**Flight Style:** Powerful and swift; occasionally soars like buteo. Legs sometimes dangle while bird is in flight. Generally spend much time perched and concealed amid vegetation.

**Voice:** High-pitched, weak *quee-quee-quee*.

**Nest:** Stick nest, lined with smaller twigs and green vegetation, placed in trees from 15 to 100 feet (4.5 to 30 meters) above ground. Nest sometimes used for several years in succession.

**Eggs:** 1 (occasionally 2 or 3) grayish-white slightly spotted with dull brown. Incubation period unknown.

**Food:** Crabs, fish, frogs, snakes, insects, rodents, and rarely birds.

**Habitat:** Riverine woodland (in North American portion of range). Elsewhere in its range prefers coastal lowlands with mixed savannah or grassland, dunes, lagoons, and ponds.

**Range:** Mexican-United States border from Arizona to Texas (locally north to Utah), south to Peru (on Pacific coast) and Guyana (on Atlantic coast); also in West Indies. Since mid-1972, small numbers of immature and adult Common Black Hawks observed and photographed in southern Florida; may have originated in Cuba or could be escapees. Unknown if species will establish itself permanently in Florida (see *American Birds,* 1976, 30:661–62).

## Golden Eagle *Aquila chrysaetos*

**Wingspread:** 75 to 94 inches (190 to 238 centimeters).
**Length:** 30 to 41 inches (76 to 104 centimeters).
**Field Recognition:** Of various subspecies only *A. c. canadensis* occurs in North America. Eagles variable in plumage; not all individuals conform exactly to age-class descriptions provided here, based on studies of Jollie (*Auk,* 1947, 64:549–76) and Spofford (*The Golden Eagle in the Trans-Pecos and Edwards Plateau of Texas,* 1964:45–46). Generally they are applicable. *Adult (five years or older)*—Large brown bird (lighter than immatures and juveniles but often black at distance or in poor light); patchy appearance formed by irregular dark and lighter brown feathers. Under favorable circumstances, and at close range, golden coloration of nape feathers seen. In some adults old, worn feathers on upperside of wings may produce white area near back; leading edge of each wing may also be whitish. Base of tail may show traces of white until bird is seven years old. Eyes hazel. Bill black. Cere, legs, and feet yellow. *Immature (second to fourth year)*—Dark brown with large, conspicuous white patch on underside of each wing but often without white patch on upperside of each wing after second year. Broad white basal tail band covers about half length of tail. Youngest birds show most white on wings and tail. *Juvenile (first year)*—Similar to immature but very dark chocolate brown or even blackish with somewhat larger white patch on underside and upperside of each wing; broad white basal tail band covers two-thirds (or more) length of tail, and black terminal band narrower than in immature. Legs feathered to toes in birds of all ages. *Chick*—Covered with white or pale gray natal down; second down thicker and white.
**Flight Style:** Soars on updrafts on broad wings, with slight dihedral. Occasional wingbeats powerful and labored.
**Voice:** Yelping *kya* or *weeo-hyo-hyo-hyo* bark.
**Nest:** Large, sometimes made of massive branch and stick, lined with sprigs of vegetation, placed in tree or on cliffs, ledges, or crags. New nests on ledges may be mere scrapes but after some years of use become impressive structures.
**Eggs:** 2 (sometimes 1 or 3) dull white blotched with brown. Incubation period in North America often about 35 days, can be as long as 43 days.

**Food:** Mammals, carrion (wild or domestic animals), occasionally birds, snakes, lizards, and fish.

**Habitat:** Mountains, canyons, foothills, farmland, and coastal areas.

**Range:** Holarctic. In North America ranges south to Mexico. There is small Appalachian and Canadian population in East. Birds from this population seen at eastern hawk-migration lookouts. Golden Eagles far more abundant in West.

## Bald Eagle *Haliaeetus leucocephalus*

**Wingspread:** 72 to 98 inches (182 to 249 centimeters).

**Length:** 30 to 43 inches (76 to 109 centimeters).

**Field Recognition:** *Adult (six years or older)*—Typical individual of subspecies *H. l. leucocephalus,* of southern United States, unmistakable with dark brown body (black at distance) and pure white head and tail. Some sixth-year birds have white heads but sprinkle of brown remains on rectrices and occasionally nape. Pattern may persist for some time. Alaskan and Canadian subspecies *H. l. alascensis* similar to southern form but larger. In all cases females larger than males. Eyes, bill, legs, and feet bright yellow. Bill larger and more robust than that of Golden Eagle. *Immatures* Bald Eagles not yet adult are extremely variable in color and patterns of plumage. Following age groups and plumage descriptions adapted from field studies of Southern (*Wilson Bulletin,* 1964, 76:121–37) and Sherrod, White, and Williamson (*Living Bird,* 1976, 15·145–46). *Sub-adult (fifth year)* Plumage similar to adults but with sprinkling of brown on most of white rectrices which may not be visible except with high magnification binoculars or telescopes. Some crown and nape feathers have brown tips; sometimes entire crown still brown. Iris yellowish. At distance, without binoculars, observers can mistake these birds for adults although head appears somewhat darker. *Late immature (fourth year)*—Body primarily brown on dorsal surface. Breast also brown but some dull white may be visible on belly. Throat light brown or whitish; sides of head and possibly forehead dull white. Crown and nape often dull white with brown-tipped feathers (sometimes largely brown). Dark brown eyeline sometimes extends ahead of and behind each eye. Bill yellow on basal half; iris brownish. *Immature (third and second years)*—In third-year birds throat has some white; breast remains brown resulting in obvious but perhaps narrow band on upper breast. Belly and lower breast whitish to white. In some birds white areas very large, in others white area small and flecked with brown. Dorsal surface dark brown mottled with occasional white patch or scattered white feathers (may have brown tips). Most common location for white back patch between wings where it resembles white V on perched bird. Coverts are often spotted with white; crown generally dark brown, but sometimes feathers have tawny tips. White may begin to show on sides of head or throat (usually throat first), but crown and nape are usually dark. Some yellow present at base of bill. Iris brown. Considerable variation in third-year plumage. In second-year birds belly and lower breast generally light tawny brown; upper breast darker, possibly with band or bib. Upper surface of body dark brown mottled with white. Sometimes few white feathers visible on belly and throat (perhaps incoming feathers of third-year plumage). Some white in tail, perhaps more than in first year. Bill and iris brown. Legs and feet yellow. *Juvenile (first year)*—Upper and lower sides of body uniformly dark brown except for occasional white portion on one or more feathers. Primaries, secondaries, and upperwing coverts dark or darker than body color, but buffy or whitish underwing lining extends outward on each wing from body toward primaries. Crown sometimes darker than rest of body. Rectrices brown, often with grayish-white varying from sprinkling to coverage of about 60 percent of central rectrices. Less white visible on dorsal side of tail. Bill horn brown. Iris light brown. Legs yellowish. *Chick*—Natal down smoky gray; second down dark brown.

**Flight Style:** Similar to Golden Eagle, but when seen approaching head-on wings may be held more level, whereas Golden Eagle frequently shows very slight dihedral in flight profile.

**Voice:** Harsh *kark-kark-kark* or *kleek-kik-ik-ik-ik-ik* cackle.

**Nest:** Massive stick structure lined with pine needles or similar softer material; located near water most of time. Nest placed high in large tree, on rocky overlook, or occasionally on ground if high supporting structures unavailable.

**Eggs:** 2 (occasionally 1 or 3) dull white. Incubation period about 35 days but subject to accurate determination.

**Food:** Fish (usually alive but sometimes as carrion); occasionally birds and mammals.

**Habitat:** Coastal areas, large rivers, lakes, and (during migration) mountain ridges.

**Range:** North America from Alaska and Canada south to Baja California and Florida.


## White-tailed Eagle *Haliaeetus albicilla*

**Wingspread:** 78 to 92 inches (198 to 233 centimeters).

**Length:** 31 to 36 inches (78 to 91 centimeters).

**Field Recognition:** Rare, robust sea eagle sometimes confused with Bald Eagle. *Adult (sexes similar)*—Typical individual of subspecies *H. a. albicilla* of Eurasia grayish-brown with yellowish-brown head (palest in worn plumage and old birds) and pure white wedge-shaped tail (sometimes rounded or square-tipped in worn plumage). Eyes, legs, and feet yellow; bill and cere pale yellow. Greenland subspecies *H. a. groenlandicus* slightly larger than *albicilla*. *Immature*—Brown, mottled with whitish on throat and breast; wings brown without whitish undersides as in immature Bald Eagle. Tail brown and wedge-tipped. In second-year birds webs of rectrices show distinctive whitish centers not present in Bald Eagles of similar age. Bill brown and larger than in Bald Eagle. Eyes brown. Cere greenish. Feet and legs yellow. *Chick*—Covered with buffy-gray down; second down coarse and dark grayish-buff.

**Flight Style:** Soars and glides on long, broad, flat wings which may show slight dihedral when thermal soaring (never as marked as in Golden Eagle). Large head extends forward in front of wings as far as tail extends behind them. Tip of tail may appear somewhat rounded when spread in soaring flight. Wingbeats shallow and rapid, usually followed by extended period of soaring and gliding.

**Voice:** Barking *gri-gri-gri* or *krick-krick-krick*. Additional calls for each sex under certain circumstances.

**Nest:** Huge stick structure lined with green vegetation and placed high in tree, on craig, or even on ground.

**Eggs:** 2 (sometimes 1 to 4) dull white. Incubation period estimated at 35 to 45 days, perhaps around 37 to 40 days.

**Food:** Fish (dead or alive), water birds, mammals, and carrion.

**Habitat:** Usually sea coasts; occasionally river valleys and inland lakes.

**Range:** Greenland, Eurasia (locally), and Africa (rarely). Extremely rare in North America, mostly Alaska. Skeletal remains found at American Harbor (Cumberland Sound), Alaska, October 1877; one immature on Unalaska (Aleutian Islands), Alaska, 5 October 1895. Two adults observed flying over Henderson Valley, Attu Island (extreme western Aleutians), Alaska, 27 May 1977, and remaining in area through 16 July 1977. Three additional Alaskan records questionable (see *Birds of Alaska*, 1959:269). Single Atlantic coast record is immature off Nantucket Lightship, Massachusetts, 14 November 1914.

## Northern Harrier (Marsh Hawk) *Circus cyaneus*

**Wingspread:** 40 to 54 inches (101 to 137 centimeters).
**Length:** 17½ to 24 inches (44 to 61 centimeters).
**Field Recognition:** Widely distributed harrier represented in North America by subspecies *C. c. hudsonius*. Individuals of all ages (except chicks) have conspicuous white rump patch. Long wings frequently form slight dihedral; wingtips generally appear pointed but occasionally can appear rounded. *Adult (male)*—Ashy gray on upperparts, white on underside with some cinnamon spots, wingtips black. Eyes orange-yellow. Cere, legs, and

feet yellow. *Adult (female)*—Brown on upperparts, lighter brown on underside with heavy brown streaks. Eyes brownish-yellow. Cere, legs, and feet yellow. *Immature male (second year)*— Brownish above but largely whitish on underside mottled with buffy markings on chest; wings and tail similar to adult male. *Immature female (second year)*—Similar to juvenile but with faint cinnamon spots on breast sometimes visible at distance. *Juvenile (both sexes)*—First-year birds similar to adult female but undersides uniformly pale cinnamon and lack spots or streaks on belly or lower chest. *Chick*—Covered with white natal down tinged with buff and dark ring around each eye; second down buffy brown.

**Flight Style:** Unsteady; frequently rocks, tips, and zigzags on updrafts. Also quarters low over marshes and fields. Sometimes hovers briefly while hunting.

**Voice:** Nasal *pee pee pee* or *chu-chu-chu* whistle.

**Nest:** Reed, grass, and small stick structure placed on ground in marshes among reeds, tall weeds, or low shrubs.

**Eggs:** 5 (sometimes 4 to 6; rarely 8 to 12) dull white or pale bluish-white occasionally slightly blotched with brown. Incubation period 23 to 31 days, often about 24 days.

**Food:** Small mammals, birds, small reptiles, frogs, insects, and crustacea.

**Habitat:** Coastal areas, freshwater and saltwater marshes, prairies, fields, and (during migration) mountain ridges.

**Range:** North America, Europe, and Asia. In North America breeds south to California, Texas, and Virginia; winters south to Cuba and (rarely) northern South America.

# Caracaras and Falcons: Falconidae

Caracaras, although related to falcons, are rather terrestrial birds and are more vulture-like than falcon-like in their habits. Falcons are long-winged raptors with pointed wingtips and long tails. They are streamlined birds with a direct and swift flight.

## Crested Caracara *Polyborus plancus*

**Wingspread:** 48 inches (122 centimeters).
**Length:** 20 to 25 inches (50 to 63 centimeters).
**Field Recognition:** Long-legged scavenger of open scrublands and prairies. *Adult (sexes similar)*—In subspecies *P. p. auduboni* of North America face red, crown and short crest black, wings and upperparts dark brown, sides of head and throat white, underparts whitish with dark brown bars, belly brownish-black,

and tail long and white with wide dark terminal band. Large light patch appears on each wing near somewhat blunt tip when bird is in flight. Eyes brown. Bill whitish but bluish at base. Legs and feet yellow. Sometimes associates with vultures. *Immature (sexes similar)*—Similar to adult but generally browner and more dingy in appearance with streaks on lower breast (rather than bars as in adults) and some light spots on upperwing coverts. *Chick*—Covered with pinkish-buff natal down, considerably darker on crown and back.

**Flight Style:** Resembles Raven's flight; irregular or zigzagging but with rapid wingbeats alternating with sailing. Appearance swift and graceful.

**Voice:** Harsh *trak-trak-trak-trak* cackle.

**Nest:** Crude structure of sticks placed in dense branches of trees, palm fronds, or cacti.

**Eggs:** 2 or 3 (rarely 4) pinkish-white to white vividly covered with reddish-brown markings. Incubation period about 28 days. May rarely deposit second clutch in same season.

**Food:** Carrion and live prey of various sorts including worms, insects, and other animals. Vegetable matter also eaten occasionally.

**Habitat:** Open scrubland and prairies.

**Range:** Central and southern Florida, southern Arizona to southern Texas, southward to Tierra del Fuego; Cuba and Isle of Pines; Falkland Islands.


## Gyrfalcon *Falco rusticolus*

**Wingspread:** 44 to 52 inches (111 to 132 centimeters).

**Length:** 20 to 25 inches (51 to 63 centimeters).

**Field Recognition:** Large Arctic falcon, variable in color, with dark and white color phases (along with variety of intermediate color forms). Wingtips generally slightly rounded compared with smaller falcons. When soaring wings usually slightly bowed or held level; occasionally dihedral seen. Gyrfalcons tend to perch on ground rather than elevated perches. *Adult male (dark phase)*—Varies from completely dark slaty blue in some birds to pale brownish-gray with much whitish marking on body and numerous tail bands. Eyes brown. Cere, legs, and feet yellow. *Adult female (dark phase)*—Somewhat larger and darker than male. *Adult male (white phase)*—Spectacular white falcon with flecks of brownish-gray on upperparts. In some birds tail barred; in others, unbarred. *Adult female (white phase)*—Similar to male but larger. *Immature (dark phase)*—Variable but many birds dark brown on upperparts with various streaks and/or spots, and lighter below with streaking. Cere, legs, and feet bluish-gray. *Immature (white phase)*—Similar to white phase adult but with some streaking on undersides. Cere, legs, and feet bluish-gray.

*Chick*—Covered with creamy-white natal down.

**Flight Style:** Slow, gull-like wingbeats as if made entirely by hands but flight deceptively fast. Often flies close to ground.

**Voice:** Harsh *kyek-kyek-kyek* or *hyaik-hyaik-hyaik;* also *ke-a-ke-a* which becomes rattling scream.

**Nest:** Merely scrape on ledge of cliff, often in gorge; old nests of Rough-legged Hawks and Ravens also used.

**Eggs:** 4 (sometimes 2 to 7) buffy or pale yellowish-white spotted with dark reds. Incubation period 28 to 29 days.

**Food:** Mainly birds such as grouse and ptarmigan but seabirds also taken frequently. Small mammals may form more of diet for immature birds during winter.

**Habitat:** Arctic coasts, mountains, tundra, and river valleys in summer. In winter along mountains, coastal regions, and other open terrain.

**Range:** Arctic portions of North America, Asia, and Europe; also Greenland and Iceland. Gyrfalcons occasionally wander southward to northern United States as rare winter visitors. Handful of records indicate these birds migrate past some eastern hawk-migration lookouts in autumn, but some reports are subject to serious question.


## Prairie Falcon *Falco mexicanus*

**Wingspread:** 40 to 42 inches (101 to 106 centimeters).

**Length:** 17 to 20 inches (43 to 51 centimeters).

**Field Recognition:** Intermediate-size falcon, similar to but slightly smaller than Peregrine Falcon. *Adult (sexes similar)*— Pale brown above, very light below with darker spots. When passing overhead black axillaries (feathers on armpits) extend outward from body almost half length of wing (much farther than shown in most field guides) and are boldly evident. Narrow brownish-black moustache on face. Eyes dark brown. Bill horn bluish, yellow at base. Cere, orbits (area around eyes), legs, and feet yellow. *Immature (sexes similar)*—Reddish-brown on upperparts, buffy on undersides marked with heavy streaks. *Chick*— Covered with pure-white natal down.

**Flight Style:** Swift, using powerful wingbeats. Occasionally soars. Generally flies at low to moderate elevations. Immature birds sometimes hover clumsily, or fly along slowly like harrier, while hunting.

**Voice:** Shrill *kik-kik-kik-kik-kik* yelp repeated frequently.

**Nest:** Scrape on ledge with overhang on cliff in foothills or abandoned stick nest of another bird.

**Eggs:** 4 or 5 (sometimes 3 to 6) pinkish-white to white heavily marked with browns or cinnamon. Incubation period 29 to 31 days.

**Food:** Small and medium-size mammals and birds often captured on ground. Occasionally lizards and insects.
**Habitat:** Cliffs and canyons in treeless country, deserts, prairies, and plains.
**Range:** Interior North America from British Columbia, Alberta, Saskatchewan, and western North Dakota south to Baja California, Arizona, New Mexico, and northern Texas.

## Peregrine Falcon *Falco peregrinus*

**Wingspread:** 38 to 46 inches (96 to 117 centimeters).
**Length:** 15 to 20 inches (38 to 51 centimeters).
**Field Recognition:** Splendid medium-size falcon now very rare throughout most of North America. *Adult (male)*—Typical individual of widespread (and endangered) North American subspecies *F. p. anatum* slaty backed and dark capped with distinctive "sideburns"; creamy underparts offset by dark narrow, horizontal bars. Subspecies *F. p. pealei,* of Pacific Northwest, may be darker and more boldly marked than *anatum*. Tundra subspecies *F. p. tundrius,* of tundra biome from treeline north to 77 degrees North latitude, smaller and paler on upperparts than other North American subspecies. Eye brown. Orbit and cere bright yellow to yellow-greenish. Bill pale bluish. Legs and feet bright yellow. *Adult (female)*—Considerably larger than adult male, and somewhat darker. *Immature*—Brown on upperparts and heavily streaked on underside (rather heavily washed with cinnamon in some females). "Sideburn" distinctive; feathering on thighs streaked vertically rather than barred horizontally as in adults. Eye brown. Orbit and cere greenish-yellow. Legs and feet greenish-yellow to bluish-gray. *Chick*—Covered with white natal down; second down longer and woolly.
**Flight Style:** Fast with quick "rowing" wingbeats. Seldom soars. Stoops at fantastic speeds.
**Voice:** Sharp *hek-hek-hek* repeated rapidly. *Witchew-witchew* in vicinity of eyrie. Some other calls.
**Nest:** Usually scrape on ledge of cliff, but occasionally ledge on tall building, or old hawk nest.
**Eggs:** 3 or 4 (sometimes 5 or 6) pinkish-white to creamy white with rich brown blotches. Incubation period 32 to 35 days.
**Food:** Mostly birds of various sizes, rarely a few mammals and other items.
**Habitat:** Cliffs overlooking rivers, open areas, tundra, coastlines, and other high places close to aquatic ecosystems. During migration appears over marshes, lakes, ponds, and rivers with concentrations of ducks, shorebirds, and other birds; also seen along mountain ridges and Atlantic and Pacific coastlines.
**Range:** Cosmopolitan. In New World occurs from Arctic south to Tierra del Fuego, but does not breed in tropics.

## Aplomado Falcon *Falco femoralis*

**Wingspread:** 40 inches (101 centimeters).

**Length:** 15 to 18 inches (38 to 45 centimeters).

**Field Recognition:** Rare, boldly marked medium-size falcon, usually seen in pairs, represented by subspecies *F. f. septentrionalis* in United States-Mexico border area. *Adult (sexes similar)*—Bluish-gray on upperparts, crown darker, head pattern distinctive with bold black line on each side of head and light stripe behind each eye. Throat white; chest nearly white, light gray, tawny, or deep cinnamon often with evenly scattered streaking. Black cummerbund on belly shows varying numbers of horizontal white bars (sometimes absent, restricted to upper and middle parts of cummerbund, or evenly distributed over entire black band). Thighs cinnamon. Tail black with five or six white bands and white tip. Eyes dark brown surrounded by yellow orbit. Bill light gray at base but blackish-gray at tip. Cere, legs, and feet yellow. *Immature (sexes similar)*—Lead gray on upper parts similar to adults, but upper breast streaked more heavily than in adults. Cummerbund rarely has white bars found on adults. Eyes brown; cere and orbit bluish-gray but gradually changes to yellow. Legs and feet yellow. *Chick*—Unknown.

**Flight Style:** Flight profile distinctive—long tail and long, narrow wings (much narrower in secondary region than in Peregrine Falcon, Prairie Falcon, or Merlin). Flight swift, graceful, and easy. Sometimes hovers when hunting, but not as easily or as long as American Kestrel. May land on ground (when in pursuit of prey) or on low scrubs.

**Voice:** High-pitched cackling; also *eek* uttered several seconds apart.

**Nest:** Old nests of other birds such as White-necked Ravens, often in yucca or mesquite.

**Eggs:** 2 or 3 (rarely 4) pale white or pinkish-white covered with blotches or spots of brown. Incubation period unknown.

**Food:** Birds, large insects, small mammals, and lizards.

**Habitat:** Open plains with mesquite, cactus, and yucca (especially *Yucca elata*).

**Range:** From United States-Mexico (Arizona, New Mexico, and Texas) border south locally to Tierra del Fuego; Trinidad. Now rare in United States; formerly more common.

## Merlin *Falco columbarius*

**Wingspread:** 23 to 26½ inches (58 to 67 centimeters).

**Length:** 10 to 13½ inches (25 to 34 centimeters).

**Field Recognition:** Small, dark, jay-size falcon. *Adult (male)*—Typical example of subspecies *F. c. columbarius,* of Alaska and southern Canada, has bluish-gray upperparts but lighter underparts with some streaking. Tail has several conspicuous black bands, bordered by narrow white bands, broader black subterminal band, and white tip. *F. c. richardsoni,* of Great Plains, paler than *columbarius. F. c. suckleyi,* of western British Columbia, very dark on back (almost black) and underparts. Eyes brown. Cere, orbit, legs, and feet yellow. Bill grayish-black. *Adult (female)*—Brown on upperparts with heavily streaked underparts. Tail brown with three or four narrow whitish bands. *Immature (sexes similar)*—Similar to adult female. *Chick*—Covered with creamy-white natal down followed by second light grayish to dark grayish-brown down.

**Flight Style:** Swift and direct with "rowing" wingbeats. Usually flies low over ground or just above treetops, providing clue to identification during migration.

**Voice:** Harsh, high-pitched *ki-ki-ki-ki-kee* uttered rapidly; other calls also used.

**Nest:** Either scrape on ground or old nest of crow placed from 5 to 60 feet (1.5 to 18 meters) above ground.

**Eggs:** 5 or 6 (sometimes 2 to 7) light buffy, covered with reddish-brown, purplish, and chocolate markings. Incubation period 28 to 32 days.

**Food:** Mostly small birds such as larks, pipits, and finches; occasionally small mammals, snakes, lizards, and other items.

**Habitat:** Forested areas, coasts, river valleys, marshes, and open areas.

**Range:** Holarctic. In North America breeds from north of treeline southward to northern California and northern Great Plains. Winters south to Ecuador and Venezuela; also West Indies.

# American Kestrel (Sparrow Hawk) *Falco sparverius*

**Wingspread:** 20 to 24½ inches (51 to 62 centimeters).

**Length:** 8¾ to 12 inches (22 to 30 centimeters).

**Field Recognition:** Our smallest and most colorful falcon (about Robin-size) *Adult (male)*—Typical individual of widely distributed North American subspecies *F. s. sparverius* has rusty back, two "sideburns" or "whiskers" on each side of head, three fairly large black patches on nape and sides of head, top of head grayish with chestnut cap, cheeks and throat white, wings bluish-gray, underparts whitish or buffy white with black spots. Tail chestnut with broad black subterminal band and narrow white tip. Individuals of subspecies *F. s. paulus,* of South Carolina south to Florida and southern Alabama, somewhat smaller than *sparverius* with fewer spots below. Eyes dark brown; cere, orbit, legs, and feet yellow. *Adult (female)*—Similar to adult male but wings brownish, back duller chestnut, underparts streaked with dark brown (not spotted). Tail duller chestnut with numerous narrow black bands. *Immature (male)*—Difficult to identify in field from adult males but generally tip of tail brownish (rather than white); more black barring on back in region of shoulders and considerable longitudinal black streaking on upper breast or chest, tending to widen into broad spots along flanks. *Immature (female)*—Extremely difficult to identify in field from adult females unless bird is in hand and examined critically. In general, however, brown and gray areas on crown or top of head less defined than in adult females (although some adults show this characteristic). Black subterminal band on tail not well defined or unusually wide (use caution when applying field mark because tips of many migrating American Kestrels broken or damaged). *Chick*—Covered with snow-white, fluffy natal down followed by thicker, dirty-white second down.

**Flight Style:** More buoyant and less direct than medium-size falcons, with occasional periods of gliding or soaring between wingbeats. Frequently hovers when hunting. When stooping wings sometimes folded into sickle shape.

**Voice:** Loud *klee-klee-klee-klee-klee* often repeated rapidly, some *chuck-chuck-chuck* calls, and sometimes other sounds.

**Nest:** Natural cavities in trees, old woodpecker holes, nest boxes, small openings in barns or other buildings, and similar locations.

**Eggs:** 4 or 5 (sometimes 2 to 7) white to pinkish-white covered with brownish spots or blotches. Incubation period 28 to 35 days, often about 31 days.

*American Kestrel eggs in nest box.*

**Food:** Small mammals, insects, occasionally small birds and other items.

**Habitat:** Urban and rural areas, deserts, prairies, wooded riverine ecosystems, agricultural areas, and other open areas.

**Range:** From treeline of North America south to Tierra del Fuego; West Indies; Falkland Islands; Juan Fernandez Islands off Chile. Generally absent from tropical forests of Amazonia.

# Hawk Identification
## and Study

During recent years much has been learned about the identification of diurnal birds of prey so that today people with little experience and a good field guide can usually recognize most of the raptors they see. It can't be stressed too strongly, however, that it is not always possible to identify every raptor. Occasionally even experts are unable to identify some birds for one reason or another.

When a diurnal raptor is seen one should remember that a number of factors determine whether the bird can be identified correctly. The most important considerations are discussed here. They include size and shape of the bird, flight style and behavior, distance of the bird from the observer, angle at which the bird is seen, prevailing light conditions, habitat in which the bird is found, range of the bird and the geographic location where the bird is seen, date and length of time the bird is observed, experience of the observer, and other factors.

## Size
One should always remember that birds of prey exhibit marked sexual dimorphism in respect to size. Usually, females are about one-third larger than males. This partly accounts for the range in wingspreads and lengths of some species. Some raptors are also sexually dimorphic in respect to color; others exhibit several strikingly different color phases.

## Shape
It is equally important to remember that a hawk's shape can vary tremendously depending upon the manner of flight being used. For example, a Broad-winged Hawk circling in a thermal will spread its wings and tail fully to achieve maximum lift. However, the same bird gliding from a thermal a few minutes later, or soaring on updrafts along a mountain, will not spread its tail and may not extend its wings fully. The result is that the bird will appear deceptively different in each situation and will cause difficulty and confusion among inexperienced hawk watchers. Therefore, it is very important to consider the shape of the bird in relation to the type of flight being used when attempting to arrive at an identification.

## Flight Style and Behavior

The flight style and behavior exhibited by a hawk are frequently critical in allowing an observer to identify the bird. Many species have distinctive flight or behavior characteristics such as peculiar wingbeats and the manner in which the wings are held. The most important of these characteristics are included in the species accounts.

## Distance from Observer

The distance at which a hawk is observed can be important in determining whether the bird can be identified correctly because it may not be possible to see essential field marks for some species at great distances. For example, if one is watching migrating hawks and sees a large, brown accipiter in the distance, the bird could be either a large, immature, female Cooper's Hawk or a small, immature, male Northern Goshawk. It might be impossible to identify the bird if it fails to come close enough to the observer to determine whether it has a conspicuous white eyebrow line. On the other hand, most migrating Ospreys can be identified at great distances because of the distinctive crooked position in which they hold their wings when soaring on updrafts along mountains and coastlines, or the distinctive bowed position of their wings when seen head-on.

## Viewing Angle

The angle at which a hawk is seen can play another important role in determining whether a bird can be identified. Looking toward the back of a bird as it flies away is the most difficult angle because few, if any, field marks are then visible. Frequently such birds can't be identified correctly. Sometimes head-on or side views can also cause difficulty when trying to identify some species.

## Light Conditions

The prevailing light conditions under which one sees a raptor are extremely important. A common species may be easy to identify in good light, but the same species may have to be considered unidentified when seen in poor light. The task is even greater when the light is bad and the bird is seen at a great distance. Caution, therefore, is always in order when looking at hawks in poor light.

Sometimes problems occur when a hawk is observed in bright sunlight. For example, if a buteo is circling overhead and viewed against the sun it is possible that "windows" will be seen in the wings. However, this does not necessarily mean that the bird is a

Red-shouldered Hawk (the species generally associated with "windows" in its wings). Almost any species can show "windows" when viewed under such conditions thus making it necessary to wait until the bird moves into a more favorable position before identifying it.

## Habitat

Except during migration, the habitat in which one sees a hawk can be a valuable clue to the bird's identity. During spring and summer, for example, a Northern Goshawk is expected to occur in forests or large tracts of woodland, an Osprey in or close to aquatic ecosystems, and an American Kestrel in farmland or other open areas. The type of habitat in which a hawk is seen will usually offer useful clues to a bird's identity.

## Range and Location

The range of a species and location where a raptor is seen offer important clues to a bird's identity. Some species are restricted to specific locations and are rarely seen elsewhere. For example, California Condors are now confined to a small portion of California, Snail Kites to southern Florida in the vicinity of the Everglades, and Zone-tailed Hawks to the southwestern border of the United States. Yet, much to the delight of birders, raptors sometimes stray from their normal ranges. Thus an immature Common Black Hawk recently appeared in Minnesota, and a Zone-tailed Hawk was photographed in Nova Scotia! Such occurrences are unusual, and one should be very skeptical and careful when attempting to identify a raptor suspected of being outside of its normal geographic range. One should also keep in mind that some strays are merely birds held in captivity by falconers and have escaped. If jesses (leather straps) are attached to the legs of the bird, they indicate it has escaped from a falconer.

## Date

The date or time of year is another factor to consider when identifying birds of prey. A much larger number of species can be expected to occur in many areas during the spring and autumn migration seasons than in the winter or summer.

## Length of Observation Period

Although it might seem obvious, the length of time a hawk is observed should also be considered when identifying a bird. The longer one can observe a bird the greater the possibility that it will be identified correctly. This can be a more important factor in some species than in others. For example, one only needs a brief glance at a Swallow-tailed Kite to determine its identity, but considerable study may be necessary to identify some immature hawks or individuals in rare color phases.

## Experience of Observer

Another important factor in determining whether a hawk can be identified correctly is the field experience of the observer. Inexperienced observers frequently make mistakes which lead to incorrect identification. For example, many novice hawk watchers mistake the white undertail coverts of many hawks for the white rump of Northern Harriers. Similarly the "windows" which appear in the wings of some hawks lead many observers to identify such birds as Red-shouldered Hawks when they may be other species. Therefore, the more field experience one has with birds of prey the less likely mistakes will be made in raptor identification.

## Miscellaneous Factors

A variety of other factors can influence one's efforts at identifying hawks. Among them are the availability, type, and magnification of the binoculars being used. Under poor light conditions, for example, an expensive pair of binoculars may enable an observer to see essential field marks which another person using binoculars of poorer quality may not be able to see. Weather conditions, including rain and snow, fog and mist, haze and air pollution, can also influence one's identification efforts, as can the opinions of one's companions. Some people have greater visual acuity than others. Thus many factors must be actively or passively considered before one can arrive at the final identification of a hawk. In most instances the process of considering these varied factors requires only a few seconds to complete, and the more experience a hawk watcher acquires the faster the process of identifying most diurnal raptors.

# Plates

Birds Perched

# Turkey Vulture

Adult

Nestling (several weeks old)

# Black Vulture

Adult

Nestling (several weeks old)

H.G.C.

47

# California Condor

Adult

# Osprey

Adult

Nestling (several weeks old)

# White-tailed Kite

Adult (at nest)

Adult (at nest)

Immature

# Swallow-tailed Kite

Adult

# Hook-billed Kite

Adult (male)

Adult (female)

# Mississippi Kite

Adult

# Snail Kite

Adults (female on left; male on right)

Nestling

Immature

# Snail Kite

A.D.C.

Adult (male)

H.G.C.

Adult (male)

# Northern Goshawk

Adult (female at nest with nestlings)

Nestlings (about 6–8 days old)

# Northern Goshawk

H.G.

Adult

# Cooper's Hawk

Adult (at nest)

Immature

# Sharp-shinned Hawk

H.M.

H.M.

# Red-tailed Hawk

Adult (*B. j. borealis*)

Adult (*B. j. calurus*)

Immature (*B. j. borealis*)

60

# Red-shouldered Hawk

Adult (*B. l. alleni*)

Adult (*B. l. lineatus*)

*B. l. elegans*

*B. l. elegans*

# Broad-winged Hawk

Adult (female) at nest with young

# Short-tailed Hawk

Adult (black phase)

# Swainson's Hawk

D.Z.

Adult

D.Z.

Juvenile

# Zone-tailed Hawk

R.A.

Adult

# White-tailed Hawk

R.A.

Adult

# Rough-legged Hawk

F.T.

Light phase

F.T.

Light phase

# Ferruginous Hawk

S.D.Z.

Adult

P.C.E./U.S.F.&W.S.

Nestlings

# Gray Hawk

Adult (top); immature (bottom)

# Harris' Hawk

Adult

Immature

69

# Common Black Hawk

R.A.

Adult (top); immature (bottom)

# Golden Eagle

Adult

# Golden Eagle

Adult

Adult

Immature

# Bald Eagle

Adult

Adult

Late Immature (4th year)

Immature (2–3 years old)

# Northern Harrier

Adult female (at nest)

Adult male

Immature

# Crested Caracara

A.D.C.

Immature

H.F.

Adult

A.D.C.

Nestling

# Crested Caracara

Adult

# Gyrfalcon

Adult (dark phase)

Adult (dark phase)

Adult (white phase)

Immature (white phase)

# Prairie Falcon

Adult (on nest)

Adult (on nest)

78

# Peregrine Falcon

Adult

Adult

# Peregrine Falcon

D.Z.

Immature

# Aplomado Falcon

D.P.H.

Adult (male)

# Merlin

# American Kestrel

B.B./Mass.D.F.&W.

Female

K.H.M.

Male

# Plates

## Birds in Flight

# Turkey Vulture

Adult (soaring on updraft)

Immature (circle of down on neck)

# Turkey Vulture

Immature (showing dihedral)

Adult

85

# Black Vulture

# California Condor

Adult (soaring)

Adult (soaring)

# California Condor

Immature (age undetermined)

Adult (landing)

# California Condor

S.R.W.

Immature (2–3 years old)

S.R.W.

Immature (1 year old)

# Osprey

Soaring

Soaring with crook in wings

# Osprey

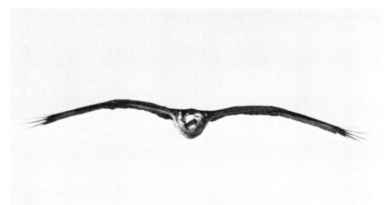

Flight profile showing bowed wings

Female

91

# Kites

White-tailed Kite (adult)

Swallow-tailed Kite

# Kites

J.C.A.

Hook-billed Kite

R.A.

Mississippi Kite (adult)

93

# Snail Kite

H.G.C.

Adult (female)

D.H.

Age undetermined

# Northern Goshawk

F.T.

Adult

F.T.

Adult

# Northern Goshawk

Adult

Immature

# Cooper's Hawk

Adult (female)

Adult (female)

# Cooper's Hawk

Immature

Immature

# Sharp-shinned Hawk

Adult

Adult

# Sharp-shinned Hawk

F.T.

Immature (eyebrow line visible)

F.T.

Immature (notched tail)

# Red-tailed Hawk

Adult (*B. j. borealis*)

H.F.

Adult (*B. j. fuertesi*)

# Red-tailed Hawk

Immature (*B. j. borealis;* hunting)

Immature (*B. j. borealis;* crop extended)

# Red-tailed Hawk

F.T.

Immature (*B. j. borealis;* hunting)

F.T.

Immature (dark phase) (*B. j. harlani*)

# Red-shouldered Hawk

Adult

Immature

# Broad-winged Hawk

F.T.

Adult

# Broad-winged Hawk

Adult

# Broad-winged Hawk

Immature

# Broad-winged Hawk

Adult (soaring in thermal)

Adult (gliding from thermal)

# Broad-winged Hawk

Kettle in thermal

Gliding from thermal

# Swainson's Hawk

Adult (light phase)

Adult (light phase)

# Rough-legged Hawk

H.G.

Dark phase (age and sex undetermined)

F.T.

Immature (light phase)

# Rough-legged Hawk

K.H.M.

Adult male (light phase)

D.Z.

Adult female (light phase)

# Rough-legged Hawk

F.T.

Adult female (light phase)

F.T.

Adult female (light phase)

113

# Short-tailed Hawk

R.A.

Adults (light phase on top; black phase on bottom)

# White-tailed Hawk

R.A.

Adult

A.D.C.

Immature

# Zone-tailed Hawk

D.Z.

Adult

D.Z.

Adult

# Zone-tailed Hawk

Adult

Adult

# Ferruginous Hawk

R.A.

Adults (normal phase on top; black phase on bottom)

# Gray Hawk

D.Z.

Adult

D.Z.

Adult

119

# Harris' Hawk

R.A.

Adult

120

# Common Black Hawk

D.Z.

Adult

D.Z.

Adult (female)

121

# Bald Eagle

Adult (6th year)

Adult

122

# Bald Eagle

F.T.

Adult

F.T.

Late Immature

123

# Bald Eagle

Immature (3rd year)

Juvenile (1st year)

124

# Golden Eagle

W.R.S.

W.R.S.

Adult

Juvenile

R.Q.

Immature

Adult

# White-tailed Eagle

E.H.

Adult

B.T.

Immature

# White-tailed Eagle

Immature

Immature

# Northern Harrier

H.G.

Adult (male)

F.T.

Adult (male)

# Northern Harrier

Adult (female)

Adult (female)

129

# Northern Harrier

F.T.

Immature (female; 2nd year)

F.T.

Juvenile

# Northern Harrier

Juvenile

Quartering over field

# Crested Caracara

Adult

# Gyrfalcon

K.E.F.

Immature

K.E.F.

Immature

133

# Peregrine Falcon

K.H.M.

Adult

W.R.S.

Adult

134

# Peregrine Falcon

A.J.

Adult (female; *F. p. anatum*)

F.R.F.

Adult (female; *F. p. anatum*)

# Aplomado Falcon

Adult (female)

Adult (female)

# Prairie Falcon

Adult

# Merlin

# American Kestrel

Adult (male; hovering)

Adult (male)

# American Kestrel

# American Kestrel

Female

# Types of Hawk Watching

Watching hawks can be separated into three basic types of activities: watching hawks migrating during spring or autumn, summer hawk watching, and winter hawk watching. The most popular of these is watching hawks migrating, but summer and winter viewing has increased in popularity in some areas.

## Watching Hawks Migrate

Hawk watchers are particularly active during the spring and autumn migration seasons because during that time the largest variety of species of diurnal birds of prey can be seen with the least amount of effort. In the East much of this activity is done from well-known raptor concentration points or hawk lookouts. And in the West, where relatively few hawk lookouts have been discovered, hawk watchers and birders often drive along roads looking for birds of prey perched on poles, wires, trees, tall shrubs, cacti, and other elevated structures. In the Southwest and probably elsewhere in the western states, raptors tend to concentrate in agricultural areas or on range with good grass, but avoid over-grazed areas of creosote bush and rabbit brush. Thus observers can concentrate their raptor-viewing efforts on productive areas and bypass poor ones. However, as new hawk lookouts are discovered in the West, they doubtless will become special gathering places for hawk watchers.

## Summer Hawk Watching

Summer hawk watching is entirely different from watching hawks migrating in spring or autumn. Since most summer activities focus on nesting birds or roadside viewing, few people spend much time watching hawks during this time. Watching nesting hawks is a sensitive activity because there is danger of causing damage to nesting efforts. Therefore, unless one is engaged in ornithological research, raptor nests should not be visited or disturbed. Nevertheless, in some instances roadside raptor viewing is possible. Sometimes other areas can be used for summer raptor viewing without disturbing the birds. In California, for example, California Condors can be seen from the Mt. Pinos Condor Observation Site from July through August; various species of diurnal birds of prey can be viewed during the summer in the Snake River Birds of Prey Natural Area in Idaho; and along parts of coastal New Jersey and in the Chesapeake Bay area of Maryland nesting Ospreys can be observed from safe distances at some locations.

## Winter Hawk Watching

Watching hawks during the winter is rapidly gaining in popularity and can be separated into two types of activities: roadside viewing and visiting raptor concentration areas. Roadside viewing is easily enjoyed by driving along rural and other lightly traveled roads looking for birds of prey perched on trees, poles, wires, or other elevated structures. American Kestrels can be seen hunting grassy areas at intersections of interstate or other highways, and some buteos also hunt along the sides of such highways in open fields.

Visiting raptor concentration areas in winter can be more rewarding especially where large numbers of Bald Eagles gather to feed in open pools of water below dams and locks on rivers such as the Mississippi and other locations. Since Bald Eagles are very sensitive to human disturbance at most winter concentration areas, they never should be approached closely. In locations such as Lake Barkley State Resort Park and the Land Between the Lakes Recreation Area in Kentucky, Reelfoot Lake State Park in Tennessee, and Glacier National Park in Montana, where formal eagle-watching programs are operated in winter, regulations assure that the birds will not be disturbed by the numerous visitors who come every year to watch them. But at other eagle concentration areas where formal viewing programs do not exist and where regulations do not prevent people from approaching the birds too closely, observers have an obligation and responsibility to remain no closer than a quarter mile (0.4 kilometer) from these birds.

# Field Equipment

Selection of the correct field equipment is essential for successful and enjoyable hawk watching. The items mentioned here are especially useful to birders interested in recreational hawk watching. Persons engaged in serious field studies of diurnal birds of prey will find additional types of equipment necessary. Some of these items are discussed further in *Autumn Hawk Flights* and various technical journals.

## Binoculars

Good binoculars are necessary for watching hawks, and birders use a wide assortment of brands and types. For most recreational hawk watching 7 × 35, 7 × 50, or 8 × 40 birding binoculars are adequate. But if more detailed field studies are planned as part of a research project, many experienced hawk watchers prefer 10X binoculars because they frequently permit more rapid and accurate hawk identification under unfavorable viewing conditions.

## Telescopes

It is useful to have a telescope available at hawk lookouts, as well as at nest sites or wintering areas, to identify birds seen at a distance or under dim light conditions. An instrument equipped with a 20X eyepiece is adequate although higher magnification is occasionally helpful. If few people are present on a lookout, the telescope can be mounted on a tripod for support. However, many experienced observers prefer to mount their telescopes on gunstocks if they intend to visit the more popular lookouts which are frequently crowded with visitors since scopes mounted on gunstocks are more maneuverable.

## Decoys

Many hawk watchers place a papier-mâché Great Horned Owl on a long pole in an upright position at the lookouts they visit. Some species of hawks such as Northern Goshawks, Sharp-shinned Hawks, and Cooper's Hawks are attracted to decoys and dart within a few feet of both decoys and observers. These can be among the most memorable experiences resulting from a visit to a lookout.

*Northern Goshawk attacking an owl decoy.*

## Field Clothing

Weather conditions at the hawk lookouts are extremely variable, and they dictate the type of field clothing which is suitable. For example, air temperatures soar into the nineties during August and September at some of the eastern lookouts, but below-freezing temperatures are not uncommon at the same lookouts during November and early December. Therefore, it is important to dress correctly.

Whenever in doubt carry an extra jacket or sweater with you on visits to the more northern lookouts. A cap for protection from the sun or a hood during the colder part of the season is also recommended. Normal hiking boots or shoes with rubber soles are ideal. Gloves, too, are necessary during cold weather. Some hawk watchers also put a raincoat or poncho into their packs.

## Other Equipment

A pack frame, knapsack, or other field pack or bag is useful when visiting a lookout because lunches, Thermoses, field guides, cameras, and other items can be carried easily while allowing free use of the hands. A pillow or cushion is useful to sit on since many mountain lookouts are covered with rocks or boulders. An aluminum beach chair can be taken to lookouts which are easily approached such as Cape May Point, New Jersey, but such chairs are not recommended for lookouts in more remote areas because of the difficulty in carrying them and the crowds that gather at some of these spots.

It is helpful to carry a small notebook or checklist on which to record the hawks and other birds you have seen. In some parks and many national wildlife refuges checklists are available without cost. Special field data forms are also used in research projects (samples are found in Appendix 4). Lunch and a beverage must be taken to most lookouts since it is impossible to buy food or beverages at most sites.

# The Migration Seasons

Hawk migrations in North America occur during fairly well defined temporal periods in the spring and autumn and are related to weather conditions, geographic features, and other factors.

## Spring Hawk Migrations

The northward spring hawk migrations in North America usually are not as spectacular or concentrated in most locations as the famous autumn flights. Nevertheless, large spring flights can be seen at a few locations, particularly along the southern shorelines of Lakes Erie and Ontario, and modest flights also occur at a number of other locations in the East including many important autumn lookouts. There are also a few locations in the West where impressive numbers of migrating hawks can be seen in spring. Perhaps the best spots are in southern Texas near the Santa Ana National Wildlife Refuge, on the Mexican border. For the most part, however, the spring hawk flights tend to be more dispersed than autumn flights.

March, April, and May are the most important months for watching hawk migrations with mid- to late April being especially important. Sometimes flights of several thousand Broadwinged Hawks are seen during a single day during that period in Texas and along the southern shoreline of Lake Ontario. In the Great Lakes region the best concentration spots seem to be located where fingers of land extend into the lake a short distance west of the lookout. In Texas various spots along the Rio Grande seem to be particularly favorable points for hawks migrating northward.

## Autumn Hawk Migrations

The autumn hawk migrations in eastern North America are among the most extraordinary animal spectacles in the world. For more than three months tens of thousands of vultures, hawks, eagles, harriers, Ospreys, and falcons follow the coastlines, mountain ridges, and Great Lakes shorelines southward en route to their ancestral wintering grounds. As they do so, they offer birders, naturalists, hawk watchers, and scientists opportunities to observe and enjoy these flights at scores of lookouts. To large numbers of out-of-doors enthusiasts, watching autumn hawk flights is a highlight of the year's activities—certainly a time to look forward to.

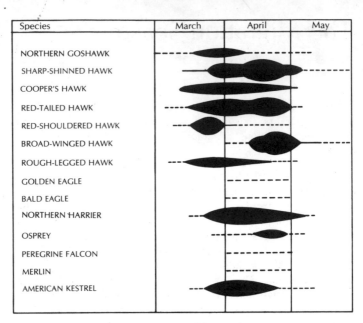

| Species | March | April | May |
|---|---|---|---|
| NORTHERN GOSHAWK | | | |
| SHARP-SHINNED HAWK | | | |
| COOPER'S HAWK | | | |
| RED-TAILED HAWK | | | |
| RED-SHOULDERED HAWK | | | |
| BROAD-WINGED HAWK | | | |
| ROUGH-LEGGED HAWK | | | |
| GOLDEN EAGLE | | | |
| BALD EAGLE | | | |
| NORTHERN HARRIER | | | |
| OSPREY | | | |
| PEREGRINE FALCON | | | |
| MERLIN | | | |
| AMERICAN KESTREL | | | |

*Spring Hawk Flights—Eastern North America*

| Species | September | October | November |
|---|---|---|---|
| TURKEY VULTURE | | | |
| NORTHERN GOSHAWK | | | |
| SHARP-SHINNED HAWK | | | |
| COOPER'S HAWK | | | |
| RED-TAILED HAWK | | | |
| RED-SHOULDERED HAWK | | | |
| BROAD-WINGED HAWK | | | |
| ROUGH-LEGGED HAWK | | | |
| GOLDEN EAGLE | | | |
| BALD EAGLE | | | |
| NORTHERN HARRIER | | | |
| OSPREY | | | |
| PEREGRINE FALCON | | | |
| MERLIN | | | |
| AMERICAN KESTREL | | | |

*Autumn Hawk Flights—Eastern North America*

148

The autumn hawk-migration season extends from early August through early December, but the bulk of the flights occur from September through November. Within this three-month period, the season can be further divided into three major segments based upon the peak migration periods of Broad-winged Hawks, Sharp-shinned Hawks, and Red-tailed Hawks. These are the three most abundant species seen at most hawk lookouts. In parts of the West the Swainson's Hawk replaces the Broad-winged Hawk in some locations, whereas in other spots both species sometimes form mixed flocks.

| Species | September | October | November |
|---|---|---|---|
| TURKEY VULTURE | | | |
| WHITE-TAILED KITE | | | |
| NORTHERN GOSHAWK | | | |
| SHARP-SHINNED HAWK | | | |
| COOPER'S HAWK | | | |
| RED-TAILED HAWK | | | |
| RED-SHOULDERED HAWK | | | |
| BROAD-WINGED HAWK | | | |
| SWAINSON'S HAWK | | | |
| ROUGH-LEGGED HAWK | | | |
| FERRUGINOUS HAWK | | | |
| GOLDEN EAGLE | | | |
| NORTHERN HARRIER | | | |
| OSPREY | | | |
| PRAIRIE FALCON | | | |
| PEREGRINE FALCON | | | |
| AMERICAN KESTREL | | | |

*Autumn Hawk Flights—Western North America*
Adapted from data supplied by Laurence C. Binford.

September is noted for Broad-winged Hawk flights which frequently peak during the middle of the month. Such flights, sometimes containing thousands of hawks, occur between 11 and 24

September, with 16 or 17 September often producing exceptional flights. At Hawk Mountain in Pennsylvania, for example, 11,392 hawks (mainly Broad-wings) were counted on 16 September 1948; similar or larger counts have been recorded at lookouts in New Jersey and at various sites along the northern shorelines of Lakes Erie and Superior.

In addition to September's spectacular Broad-wing flights, Bald Eagles migrate southward in small numbers during late August and throughout September, with occasional stragglers appearing in December. Ospreys are notable components of the September hawk flights, the largest numbers appearing during mid- to late September. On 11 September 1965, for example, a flight of 102 Ospreys passed Bake Oven Knob, Pennsylvania.

October is the second important period in the autumn hawk-migration season. Sharp-shinned Hawks are the most abundant migrants from early to mid-October, but they become less numerous later in the month. Adding zest to the season, however, are lesser numbers of other species including Northern Goshawks, Cooper's Hawks, Golden Eagles, Northern Harriers, Peregrine Falcons, Merlins, and American Kestrels. On 16 October 1970, at Cape May Point, New Jersey, an extraordinary flight of about 25,000 American Kestrels was seen! In addition to hawks, thousands of Canada Geese are seen during October at the hawk lookouts; thrushes, kinglets, vireos, wood warblers, blackbirds and grackles, and finches and sparrows are also seen.

From the end of October to early November, the largest and most majestic hawks reach peaks of abundance in their southward migrations. On any cold day with northwest winds in early November large numbers of Red-tailed Hawks are likely to be seen at many of the mountain lookouts—especially in the East. Adding more excitement to these flights are lesser numbers of Northern Goshawks, Red-shouldered Hawks, Rough-legged Hawks, Golden Eagles, Northern Harriers, and occasionally other species. Golden Eagles are the highlights of the eastern hawking season. Indeed every visitor to an eastern hawk lookout hopes to see one of these regal birds, although less than 55 are counted each year even at the best lookouts in the East. And although these birds are very common in many western locations, they are no less spectacular. Nevertheless, dedicated eastern hawk watchers can see Golden Eagles eventually if they make repeated visits to places such as Bake Oven Knob and Hawk Mountain in Pennsylvania. Perhaps you will be lucky on your first visit and see a Golden Eagle immediately. If you select the correct day in mid- to late October or early November, it is possible to do so. And if you fail on your first trip, try again. To see the King of Birds is worth the effort!

# Mechanics of Hawk Flights

In addition to knowing when to visit a hawk lookout during the migration seasons, the chances of seeing a good hawk flight are improved through an understanding of the basic mechanics of hawk flying. Among the most important factors are weather conditions, especially local weather conditions such as updrafts and thermals, and so-called diversion-lines or leading-lines.

## General Weather Conditions

During springtime in the East, the largest hawk flights seem to occur on southerly winds accompanied by a drop in barometric pressure, a rise in air temperature, and the westerly approach of a low-pressure area and a cold front. In the West, particularly in the Rio Grande area of Texas, large concentrations of northward migrating hawks sometimes develop along parts of the Texas border when strong northerly winds occur.

Large autumn hawk flights also tend to occur in the wake of certain weather features. This is particularly true in the East; a pronounced low-pressure area first covers lower New England and upstate New York followed a day or two later by the passage of a strong cold front across the East or Northeast. The front is accompanied by brisk northwest, north, or west winds. This combination of wind and weather usually produces ideal hawk flight conditions, but occasionally good flights also occur on easterly and southerly winds.

## Updrafts

The cold, brisk, northwest surface winds which usually occur after the passage of a strong cold front create excellent flight conditions for migrating hawks because they strike the sides of mountains and are deflected upward. These updrafts or deflective air currents are perfect for the soaring flight used by buteos, accipiters, and other hawks. In addition to creating strong updrafts along the inland mountains, northwest winds tend to concentrate hawks at certain geographic bottlenecks such as Cape May Point, New Jersey. Apparently the hawks are unwilling to cross Delaware Bay unless the wind changes direction. However, they sometimes follow the New Jersey side of the bay northward until they can cross at a narrow spot despite the northwesterly winds. At other times under northwesterly wind conditions, hawks tend to make large circles in the vicinity of Cape May Point and are counted repeatedly as they circle the tip of the cape. Such activity provides excellent recreational hawk-

*When surface winds strike the sides of mountains they are deflected upward. Migrating hawks soar on these updrafts.*

watching opportunities but makes it difficult to make accurate counts of the birds. When the wind changes direction, however, the birds readily cross Delaware Bay and continue their southward migrations.

### Lee Waves

Lee waves, undulatory movements of air downwind from an obstacle such as a mountain, apparently are used by migrating hawks at times, but not much is known about the relationship of these local weather features to hawk migrations.

### Thermals

Thermals (bubbles of warm air rising into the atmosphere) are also important to migrating Broad-winged Hawks and Swainson's Hawks. Indeed it is this dependence upon thermals which causes hundreds of Broad-wings, for example, to gather in milling flocks called "kettles"—extraordinary spectacles which hawk watchers eagerly look forward to.

In the eastern United States and Canada, Broad-winged Hawks are the only raptors which make extensive use of thermals during migration. But in the West, Swainson's Hawks also use thermals extensively, and both species sometimes kettle in mixed flocks in Central America en route to or from their winter ranges.

*Migrating Broad-winged Hawks and Swainson's Hawks enter thermals, ride them aloft, then glide downward to another thermal and repeat the process.*

The use of thermals by hawks enables these birds to migrate over vast distances while expending very little energy. This is accomplished by entering thermals and remaining in them as they rise into the atmosphere. When the warm air in the thermals begins to cool and the thermals dissipate in the form of cumulus clouds, the hawks leave and begin long, downward glides sometimes extending for several miles until another thermal is located. Then the process is repeated. In this manner Broad-winged Hawks migrate cross-country drifting on the wind, or they move down the great folds of the Appalachians or around the shorelines of the Great Lakes, thence around the Gulf of Mexico and through Central America into their South American winter range.

Thermal soaring is one of the most effective and practical methods of flight employed by migrating hawks. Sometimes Broad-winged Hawks also use combinations of thermal and updraft soaring, as do other species, when cross-country flights are taken over mountains and valleys. At such times hawks may drift across valleys on thermals, but may change direction and use updrafts along mountains when they are encountered, before resorting to thermal soaring.

## Thermal Streets

Under certain conditions thermals and wind combine to produce long parallel lines of thermals and clouds called thermal streets. Migrating hawks can soar and glide in lines extending several miles in length along these streets, although use of thermal streets is probably relatively uncommon.

## Squall Lines

Occasionally migrating hawks soar on updrafts occurring in front of squall lines. The squalls are neighboring thunderstorms arranged in a line parallel to, and in front of, an advancing cold front. In one instance about 4,300 hawks were observed soaring on updrafts in front of an advancing squall line.

## Diversion-Lines

In various parts of eastern North America, prominent geographic features such as the shorelines of the Great Lakes, the Appalachian Mountain ridges, and the Atlantic coastline extend unbroken for long distances. Scientists refer to these natural features as diversion-lines or leading-lines. When soaring hawks

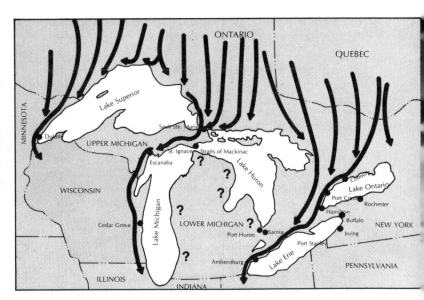

*Some migrating hawks follow prominent geographic features such as shorelines of large lakes, mountain ridges, or coastlines when they are encountered. Such natural features are called diversion-lines or leading-lines.*

encounter such diversion-lines during migration, they frequently divert at least a portion of their migration along such features for varying distances. For birds such as the Broad-winged Hawk, which is especially reluctant to cross large expanses of water, the northern and western shorelines of the Great Lakes act as major autumn diversion-lines. In the spring, when the hawks are migrating northward, the southern shorelines of Lakes Erie and Ontario play a similar role. Elsewhere, as along the ridges of the Appalachians, the updrafts provide favorable soaring conditions for buteos and a wide assortment of other hawks. Falcons, however, are not particularly dependent upon soaring flight and occur in much larger numbers during autumn along the Atlantic coastline rather than inland along the ridges. Many of these migrating falcons take advantage of the large numbers of small birds, which also migrate along the coast, as a readily available food supply.

Although scientists differ sharply about the role wind drift plays in influencing migrating hawks to use diversion-lines—some think hawks follow them regardless of wind conditions, others because of wind conditions—in all probability a combination of both factors, especially strong northwest winds and prominent geographic features, influence migrating hawks to utilize diversion-lines. Like many aspects of hawk migrations, however, additional field studies may produce a more refined understanding of diversion-line phenomena.

# Hawk Migration Lookouts

# United States

## Alabama

### Dauphin Island (near Mobile)

**Spring Flights:** Information unavailable.
**Autumn Flights:** Fair.
**Description:** A hook-shaped barrier beach island in the Gulf of Mexico just south of Mobile.
**Access:** From Mobile drive south on State Route 163 across the causeway and bridge to the eastern part of Dauphin Island. Details are unavailable regarding the best hawk-watching spots, but exposed areas near the eastern end of the island presumably are satisfactory. Such spots include the dunes along the Gulf, the Audubon Bird Sanctuary, and the Indian shell-mound area on the bay side of the island which is less than a mile (1.6 kilometers) wide.
**References:** *American Birds,* 1971, 25 (3):539–40; *Alabama Birds* (University of Alabama Press, 1976).

### Fort Morgan State Park

**Spring Flights:** Information unavailable.
**Autumn Flights:** Fair.
**Description:** The western end of a narrow peninsula projecting westward from the eastern side of Mobile Bay. Hawk watching is done anywhere on the bay side of the park. The migrating hawks approach from the east in autumn and sometimes kettle overhead before crossing the bay to Dauphin Island on the western side of the bay.
**Access:** From Interstate 10 running between Pensacola, Florida, and Mobile, Alabama, drive south on Route 59 to Gulf Shores. At the junction of Routes 59 and 180 turn right (west) onto Route 180 and continue for about 21 miles (33.6 kilometers) to the end of the road. The last mile (1.6 kilometers) is in Fort Morgan State Park. Additional information on hawk watching within the park may be available from park officials.
**References:** *NHMA,* 1976, 1 (2):9; *Alabama Birds* (University of Alabama Press, 1976).

# California

## Pt. Diablo Lookout (near San Francisco)

**Spring Flights:** Fair.
**Autumn Flights:** Excellent.
**Description:** Two 900-foot (270 meters) hills (Cross Hill and Bunker Hill) located 0.4 mile (0.6 kilometer) apart, but connected by a saddle-like ridge, overlooking the mouth of San Francisco Bay. *Cross Hill,* the northeastern site, has a broad, flat parking lot at its summit along with what looks like a cross. It is best used for watching spring hawk migrations. *Bunker Hill,* the southwestern site, has numerous cement bunkers and platforms on its summit and is the best spot from which to watch autumn hawk migrations.
**Access:** From San Francisco follow U.S. 101 north across the Golden Gate Bridge. Upon leaving the bridge, take the Alexander Avenue exit toward Sausalito, but rather than continue directly to that town, proceed only about 50 yards (45 meters) and turn left under U.S. 101 as if returning to San Francisco. Just before rejoining U.S. 101, turn right uphill on a paved road into the Golden Gate National Recreation Area (G.G.N.R.A.). Proceed 1.2 miles (1.9 kilometers) to the first Y intersection. To reach Cross Hill, park here and walk about 50 yards (45 meters) down the right-hand road to a narrow dirt road that goes to the top of the hill at the "cross"; this road is closed to motorized vehicles and presents a steep walk. To reach Bunker Hill, drive left at the Y intersection 0.6 mile (0.9 kilometer) to the first crest, where a sign announces "Begin one-way road" (in the direction you are going). Park here and walk several hundred yards up a narrow gated road to the highest point of the northeast end.

"From the north on U.S. 101, the Alexander Avenue exit is not marked as such, but is called simply 'Sausalito'; another sign points to the G.G.N.R.A. There are other Sausalito exits, but this is the only one in sight of the Golden Gate Bridge. Immediately upon leaving the highway, turn left onto the same G.G.N.R.A. road [just] described."
**Reference:** *Birding,* 1977, 9 (1):29–30.

# Connecticut

## Audubon Center of Greenwich

**Spring Flights:** Information unavailable.
**Autumn Flights:** Excellent.
**Description:** An exposed area directly across from the center's lodge and adjacent to the main driveway. This site may be most useful for watching Broad-winged Hawk migrations.

**Access:** From New York, or points north, follow Interstate 684 to Exit 3 (or Exit 3-N if coming from the south), leave the highway there and continue north on Route 22 to a traffic light. Turn right onto Route 433 and continue 2 miles (3.2 kilometers) to John Street. The Audubon Center is on the corner.

If arriving via the Merritt Parkway leave the parkway at Exit 28 (Round Hill Road), continue north on Round Hill Road for 1.4 miles (2.2 kilometers) to John Street. Turn left and drive 1.4 miles (2.2 kilometers) to the corner of Riversville Road and the center.

Those approaching via Interstate 95 (Connecticut Turnpike), leave the turnpike at Exit 3 and turn onto Arch Street. Immediately after passing the Railroad Avenue traffic light turn left onto Soundview Drive and continue to Field Point Road. Turn right onto Field Point Road and continue to Brookside Drive (the first left). Turn onto Brookside Drive and proceed 0.6 mile (0.9 kilometer) to Glenville Road. Turn left and drive to Glenville. Turn right at the traffic light onto Riversville Road and proceed 4.4 miles (7 kilometers) to John Street. The center is on the corner.

This facility is open Tuesday through Saturday (9:00 A.M. to 5:00 P.M.); closed Sunday, Monday, and holiday weekends. When autumn hawk watches occur on holiday weekends special arrangements are made to allow hawk watchers entrance to the center. For more information write to the Audubon Center at 613 Riversville Road, Greenwich, Conn. 06830.
**References:** *NI IMA,* 1976, 1 (2):5; 1977, 2 (2):9.

## Bald Peak (near Salisbury)

**Spring Flights:** Information unavailable.
**Autumn Flights:** Good.
**Description:** A rocky ridge with a 360-degree view.
**Access:** From Hartford drive north on Route 44 to Salisbury (in the northwest corner of the state), then follow Mount Riga Road for about 4.1 miles (6.5 kilometers) to the Bald Peak parking area (about 0.3 mile or 0.5 kilometer beyond South Pond). Five minutes are required to walk from the parking area to a large rock ledge.
**References:** *AHF; GEHW.*

## Bluff Head (in North Guilford)

**Spring Flights:** Poor.
**Autumn Flights:** Excellent.
**Description:** A rocky bluff rising some 350 feet (105 meters) above the surrounding deciduous forests with unrestricted visibility from the north through the south, but with visibility toward the west blocked by woodland.

**Access:** From Exit 58 off the Connecticut Turnpike (Interstate 95) in Guilford, drive north on Route 77. At 4.3 miles (6.8 kilometers) cross Route 80 and continue north on Route 77. At 6.9 miles (11 kilometers) Lake Quonapoug will be seen on the right. At 8.5 miles (13.6 kilometers) you will pass Great Hill Road on the left. From this junction go 0.3 mile (0.4 kilometer); on the left an unpaved parking area will be seen beneath large pine trees. Park here and take the blue trail (brazes on trees) up the steep talus slope. This path leads about 1.5 miles (2.4 kilometers) to the top of Bluff Head. The trail is very steep at the start up the talus, and several overlooks will be passed before the final summit is reached.

**Reference:** *NHMA,* 1976, 1 (2):4–5.

## Chestnut Hill (Litchfield)

**Spring Flights:** Poor.
**Autumn Flights:** Good.
**Description:** A large open farm field with unobstructed views from the north through the south.
**Access:** At the Watertown exit of Interstate 84 near Waterbury, drive north on Route 63 through Watertown and continue north on Route 63 for another 11.5 miles (18.4 kilometers), past the blinker light at Morris, to Camp Dutton Road (south of Litchfield Center). Turn right onto Camp Dutton Road and drive for a mile (1.6 kilometers) to the end of the road at Chestnut Hill Road. Park on Chestnut Hill Road and observe from here.
**Reference:** None.

## Lighthouse Point Park (in New Haven)

**Spring Flights:** Poor.
**Autumn Flights:** Good (sometimes excellent).
**Description:** A large, open field atop a knoll about 300 yards north of the park's beach.
**Access:** From Interstate 95 at New Haven, take Exit 50 (Main Street East Haven) and at the second traffic light turn right onto Townsend Avenue. Continue on Townsend Avenue 2.2 miles (3.5 kilometers) to the traffic light at Lighthouse Point Road. Turn right and follow Lighthouse Point Road for 0.1 mile (0.1 kilometer) into the park. Park in the unpaved parking lot. Then walk north to the large field atop the knoll adjacent to the parking lot from which observations are made.
**References:** *Auk,* 1895, 12:259–70; *GEHW.*

## Taft School (in Watertown)

**Spring Flights:** Poor.
**Autumn Flights:** Good.
**Description:** The open athletic fields of the Taft School.
**Access:** From Interstate 84 near Waterbury take the Watertown exit and drive north on Route 63 for 5 miles (8 kilometers) to Watertown. At the stoplight and junction with Route 6 turn left onto Route 6 and follow it west for less than a mile (about 1.6 kilometers) past the Taft School (on the right) to Guernseytown Road. Turn right onto the road and drive for 0.1 mile (0.1 kilometer). Then turn right again into a large parking lot. Park here and walk east for another 0.1 mile (0.1 kilometer) to the top of a hill overlooking the Taft School. Observe from here.
**Reference:** *NHMA*, 1976, 1 (2):5.

# Delaware

## Brandywine Creek State Park (near Wilmington)

**Spring Flights:** Information unavailable.
**Autumn Flights:** Fair.
**Description:** A stone wall overlooking the Brandywine Creek and adjacent to the main parking lot in the park.
**Access:** From Wilmington, 3 miles (4.8 kilometers) to the south, drive north on Route 100 to the junction with Route 92. Enter the park. Then continue to the main parking lot and stone wall adjacent to it. Observe from there.
**Reference:** *Delaware Conservationist,* 1969, 13 (4):3–13.

# Florida

## Canaveral National Seashore (near Titusville)

**Spring Flights:** Information unavailable.
**Autumn Flights:** Fair (occasionally good to excellent).
**Description:** The top of the old NASA camera pad No. 10 from which observers have clear views over the coast and surrounding barrier beach island. In October, Sharp-shinned Hawks and Peregrine Falcons migrate past the spot. Occasionally other species are seen.
**Access:** From Interstate 95 near Titusville, drive east on State Route 402 for about 12 miles (19.2 kilometers) to Playalinda Beach at the southeastern end of Canaveral National Seashore.

Once there drive north on the beach road for about 5 miles (8 kilometers) to the camera pad near the end of the road. Drive onto the pad and observe from there. Bird watchers are allowed on the pad despite the sign asking people to stay off. However, check with the park ranger before using the pad because it still is an active NASA facility.
**Reference:** None.


## Destin

**Spring Flights:** Information unavailable.
**Autumn Flights:** Fair.
**Description:** A vantage point behind a shopping center.
**Access:** From Destin drive to a point along U.S. Route 98 just before the highway meets the bridge crossing East Pass. The shopping center is located along the north side of the highway. Park and walk to the vantage point behind the center. Observe from there.
**Reference:** None.


## Gulf Breeze

**Spring Flights:** None.
**Autumn Flights:** Fair.
**Description:** The side of a road at a sharp curve.
**Access:** From Pensacola drive south on Route 98 into Gulf Breeze. Continue to the traffic light (the only one in town), turn west at the light onto Fairpoint Drive, and continue 1.7 miles (2.7 kilometers) until the road curves sharply toward the southeast. Observe from the roadside in the vicinity of the curve. Hawks approach from the east.
**References:** *JHMA,* 1975, 1 (1):30, 32; *GEHW.*


## Key West Area

**Spring Flights:** Information unavailable.
**Autumn Flights:** Good (sometimes excellent).
**Description:** Probably no specific site in the Key West area can be recognized as a hawk lookout, although kettles of Broad-winged Hawks are seen occasionally over the Key West area in autumn (October). Birders should remain alert and look for these hawk flights from time to time.
**Access:** From the southern Florida mainland drive south on U.S. Route 1 to Key West.
**Reference:** *AHF.*

## Port Canaveral (near Cocoa)

**Spring Flights:** Information unavailable.
**Autumn Flights:** Poor to fair.
**Description:** An exposed area facing north along a ship channel at the north end of Jetty Park (when hawks are flying along the beach), or a spot along the ship channel about 0.25 mile (0.4 kilometer) west of the park (when hawks are flying inland from the beach). Accipiters and falcons form most of the flights seen at these spots.
**Access:** From Interstate 95 just north of Cocoa drive east on State Route 528 for about 10 miles (16 kilometers) to a toll plaza. Pass through the plaza and continue on Route 528 for about 2 miles (3.2 kilometers) more to the Port Canaveral sign. Turn left and continue a short distance to George J. King Boulevard. Then turn right onto the boulevard and drive for about a mile (1.6 kilometers) to a "Jetty Park" sign. Follow the sign to the park and continue to the ship channel at the north end of the park. Stop there and observe or move westward along the channel if the hawks are flying somewhat inland from the beach.
**Reference:** None.

## South Ponte Vedra Beach

**Spring Flights:** Poor.
**Autumn Flights:** Poor to fair.
**Description:** A semi-permanent sand dune (elevation 20 feet; 6 meters) partly covered with grass and providing observers with a view of the Atlantic Ocean on the east and a large marsh on the west. This site has very limited value, but sizable flights of falcons (chiefly American Kestrels with a few Merlins and Peregrine Falcons) occur occasionally in mid-April.
**Access:** From the junction of U.S. Route 90 and State Route A-1-A in Jacksonville Beach drive south on Route A-1-A for 12.7 miles (20.3 kilometers) to the hawk-watching site. About 3.1 miles (4.9 kilometers) before reaching the site Mickler's Landing Road crosses the highway on which you are driving. The site itself can be recognized by a scattered grove of dead palm trees on the west side of the highway and the high dune on the east side.
**Reference:** *NHMA*, 1976, 1 (1):3; 1977, 2 (2):11.

## St. George Island Hawk Lookout (near Apalachicola)

**Spring Flights:** Poor.
**Autumn Flights:** Fair.

**Description:** The top of a 50-foot-high (15 meters) sand dune at the end of a wooded area near the eastern end of St. George Island. Unrestricted views are enjoyed in all directions, and hawks normally fly eastward within easy viewing distance.

**Access:** From Apalachicola drive east on U.S. Route 98 for about 5 miles (8 kilometers) toward Eastpoint. Then turn south and continue for about 5 miles (8 kilometers) on an unnumbered road and causeway to St. George Island. Once on the island drive east (left) on the only paved road for about 12 miles (19.2 kilometers) to a point where trees end abruptly adjacent to some very large sand dunes. The last (and largest) dune, known locally as Sugar Hill, is used as the hawk lookout.

**Reference:** *NHMA,* 1977, 2 (2):11–12.


## St. Joseph Peninsula

**Spring Flights:** Information unavailable.

**Autumn Flights:** Fair.

**Description:** A high, sandy hammock on a peninsula 18 miles (28.8 kilometers) long and about 0.25 mile (0.4 kilometer) wide from which observers have uninterrupted views of the Gulf of Mexico toward the west and St. Joseph Bay toward the east. Accipiters are the predominant hawks observed.

**Access:** At the junction of Route 71 and U.S. Route 98 in Port St. Joe (20 miles or 32 kilometers west of Apalachicola) turn east onto U.S. Route 98 and continue approximately 1.5 miles (2.4 kilometers) to Route 30 (identified by a large sign pointing to St. Joseph Peninsula State Park). Turn right onto Route 30 and continue about 6 miles (9.6 kilometers) to Route 30E (marked by another park sign). Follow Route 30E toward the park for about 6 more miles (9.6 kilometers) until you arrive at the Sunland Park for the Handicapped. Then continue on Route 30E about 0.5 mile (0.8 kilometer) past this area to the first spot where the bay and Gulf are visible. Observe from there.

**Reference:** *NHMA,* 1976, 1 (2):8–9.


## Upper Plantation Key

**Spring Flights:** Information unavailable.

**Autumn Flights:** Fair.

**Description:** An open area with adequate views outside the building occupied by the research department of the National Audubon Society.

**Access:** From the southern Florida mainland drive south on U.S. Route 1 to Travernier on Upper Plantation Key. Then drive to the National Audubon Society office at 115 Indian Mound Trail. Additional information may be available from Audubon officials.

**Reference:** *AHF.*

# Georgia

## Cumberland Island National Seashore (near St. Marys)

**Spring Flights:** Information unavailable.
**Autumn Flights:** Poor.
**Description:** A barrier beach island along which migrating Peregrine Falcons, Merlins, American Kestrels, and other raptors stop to rest and feed. Although the overall rating for this site is poor, as many as 93 Peregrine Falcons have been reported in one season along the beaches (chiefly the first two weeks in October). The stone jetty at the southern end of the island is a suitable observation point as well as the middle and northern sections of the beaches.
**Access:** From the junction of Interstate 95 and State Route 40 near Kingsland, follow State Route 40 eastward to St. Marys where a National Park Service passenger ferry (toll) transports visitors to Cumberland Island. Since the schedule for departure may vary current information is available from the Cumberland Island National Seashore, P.O. Box 806, St. Marys, Ga. 31558. Upon reaching the island and the visitors' center, one can walk to the middle or northern sections of the beaches to look for falcons or walk 3.5 miles (5.6 kilometers) south to the rock jetty and observe from there. However, special care should be taken not to walk on the dunes to prevent dune damage. Overnight camping is permitted at selected sites on the island by reservation. Details can be secured from park headquarters.
**Reference:** None.

# Illinois

## Illinois Beach State Park (near Waukegan)

**Spring Flights:** Information unavailable.
**Autumn Flights:** Fair.
**Description:** The south shore of Lake Michigan from which observers have exposed views of hawks.
**Access:** From Waukegan drive north on State Route 42 (Sheridan Road) for 4.5 miles (7.2 kilometers). Then turn right onto Beach Road and continue into the park. The Lake Michigan shore is reached via a nature trail from a parking lot in the Nature Preserve portion of the southern section of the park. Additional details may be available from park authorities.
**Reference:** *GBF.*

# Indiana

## Indiana Dunes National Lakeshore (near Michigan City)

**Spring Flights:** Good (sometimes excellent).
**Autumn Flights:** None.
**Description:** The top of a bare dune known locally as Mount Baldy. Hawks follow an east-to-west direction with Sharp-shinned Hawks and Red-tailed Hawks being observed most commonly in late March and April.
**Access:** From Michigan City drive west on U.S. Route 12 for a few miles to the Mount Baldy Area of the National Lakeshore. Park in the parking area closest to Mount Baldy, then walk along the trail leading to the top of Mount Baldy from which hawk watching is done. Maps of the area are available at the federal information center located along U.S. Route 12 a few miles west of the Mount Baldy Area.
**Reference:** None.

## Indiana Dunes State Park (near Michigan City)

**Spring Flights:** Good (sometimes excellent).
**Autumn Flights:** None.
**Description:** The top of Mount Tom or the south rim of the Beachhouse Blowout. Hawks follow an east-to-west direction with Sharp-shinned Hawks and Red-tailed Hawks being observed most commonly in late March and April.
**Access:** From Michigan City drive west on U.S. Route 12 for several miles past the Mount Baldy Area of Indiana Dunes National Lakeshore to the entrance to Indiana Dunes State Park (an entrance fee is charged). Obtain a park map at the entrance, then drive to the parking lot near Mount Tom on Trail 8. Park there, then walk to the top of Mount Tom from which hawk watching is done. Alternatively, drive to the parking lot along the beach, then walk east on Trail 10 along the beach to the blowout. Observe from there.
**Reference:** None.

# Kentucky

Although hawks migrate across Kentucky, limited information is available regarding consistently used concentration points and flight lines. In *The Birds of Kentucky* (American Ornithologists' Union, 1965), however, Robert M. Mengel mentions that Red-tailed Hawks migrate down the Mississippi Valley in early November.

# Maine

## Acadia National Park (near Bar Harbor)

**Spring Flights:** Information unavailable.
**Autumn Flights:** Fair.
**Description:** The exposed summit of Mount Cadillac or the flat ground between the ocean and the base of Mount Cadillac near Otter Creek.

*Frenchman's Bay seen from the summit of Mount Cadillac, Acadia National Park, Maine.*

**Access:** From Bar Harbor drive into the park and follow the directional signs to the site you select. Other roads also lead to the park from different directions. The route to the top of Mount Cadillac is well marked.
**References:** *AHF; GEHW.*

## Bradbury Mountain State Park (near Freeport)

**Spring Flights:** Information unavailable.
**Autumn Flights:** Good.
**Description:** A bare granite mountaintop providing hawk watchers with excellent views of migrating birds. Mid-September to mid-October appears to be the best hawk-watching period.

**Access:** From the town of Pownal drive north on Route 9 for a short distance to the park entrance. Alternatively from Durham drive south on Route 9 for several miles (kilometers) to the park entrance. Enter and drive to the main parking lot near the top of the mountain. Park there, then make a short 10-minute hike to the mountaintop following directional signs.
**Reference:** None.

## Casco Bay Area (near Portland)

**Spring Flights:** Information unavailable.
**Autumn Flights:** Good.
**Description:** Detailed information on lookouts in this area is unavailable. However, the best hawk lookout in the Casco Bay area apparently is located on private property near Harpswell. Observations elsewhere along the shoreline of Casco Bay (particularly near the head of the bay) and on the outer islands may also produce favorable flight lines and suitable lookouts.
**Access:** Various roads lead to the Casco Bay area near Portland. Refer to local road maps.
**References:** *American Birds,* 1974, 28 (1):113–14; *NHMA,* 1976, 1 (2):5; *GEHW.*

## Monhegan Island

**Spring Flights:** Information unavailable.
**Autumn Flights:** Fair.
**Description:** The top of an open field near the eastern shore, beyond the last buildings of the village, where the island's only main road ends. Sharp-shinned Hawks pass overhead.
**Access:** From the wharf follow the main road to the right. Continue through the village and along the harbor, then continue on the road as it turns inland and eventually ends at the top of the field near the eastern shore.
**Reference:** *Bird Islands Down East* (Macmillan, 1941:114).

## Mount Agamenticus (near Ogunquit)

**Spring Flights:** Information unavailable.
**Autumn Flights:** Fair.
**Description:** A fire tower on the summit of Mount Agamenticus from which hawk watchers have good views of passing birds.
**Access:** From the center of Ogunquit drive south on U.S. Route 1 for 0.4 mile (0.6 kilometer) to Agamenticus Road. Turn right (west) onto Agamenticus Road and continue about 2 miles (3.2 kilometers) to a stop sign. Turn right and drive a short distance to Mountain Road on the left. Turn onto Mountain Road and continue 1.5 miles (2.4 kilometers), then turn right onto a road and

continue 0.6 mile (0.9 kilometer) to a large parking area on the summit of the mountain. Park there and observe from the nearby fire tower. The distance from U.S. Route 1 to the mountain summit is about 6.1 miles (9.1 kilometers).
**Reference:** None.

# Maryland
## Assateague Island National Seashore
**Spring Flights:** Information unavailable.
**Autumn Flights:** Fair.
**Description:** The dunes and outer beach areas along the length of the island are famous as a Peregrine Falcon flyway.
**Access:** There are two entrances to Assateague Island National Seashore. To reach the northern entrance drive west on Route 50 from Ocean City to the junction of Route 611. Turn onto Route 611 and continue south for a few miles (kilometers) until park signs and an unnumbered road leading east into the park are encountered. The southern entrance (located in Virginia) is reached from Pocomoke City, Maryland, by driving south on Route 13 to Route 175, then turning east onto Route 175 and following it into the park.
**References:** *Raptor Research News*, 1971, 5:31–43; *Journal Wildlife Management*, 1972, 36:484–92.

## Bay Hundred Peninsula (near Fairbank)
**Spring Flights:** None.
**Autumn Flights:** Fair.
**Description:** A narrow peninsula extending southward into Chesapeake Bay with largely rural land either wooded or under cultivation.
**Access:** From Easton follow Route 33 west to St. Michaels, then west and south on the Bay Hundred Peninsula to its tip near the village of Fairbank. Hawk watching is done from Route 33 near the southern tip of the peninsula anywhere adjacent to open habitats with good visibility. Do not trespass!
**Reference:** None.

## Dan's Rock Hawk Lookout (near Midland)
**Spring Flights:** Information unavailable.
**Autumn Flights:** Good.
**Description:** A rocky outcropping near a fire tower with a spectacular view of the Potomac River valley, good views extending from the northeast through the southeast, and less satisfactory views in other directions.

**Access:** From Frostburg drive south on Route 36 to Midland. Upon entering Midland turn left onto the first paved road. Continue on this road crossing two small metal bridges to the second paved road on the left (Dan's Rock Road). Turn onto this road and continue for about 3 miles (4.8 kilometers) to the end of it. The rocky outcropping and fire tower will be seen. The lookout rocks are about 150 feet (45 meters) from the road near the base of the tower. Inquire in Midland for more specific directions to the spot.

**Reference:** None.

## Hooper Island (near Church Creek)

**Spring Flights:** None.
**Autumn Flights:** Good.
**Description:** An island group consisting of three long, narrow islands (Upper, Middle, and Lower Hooper islands) bordered on the east by the Honga River and on the west by Tar and Chesapeake bays. Hawk watching can be done at various spots on the three-part island and observers will sometimes find it necessary to drive down the island-group looking for migrating birds in various directions. At other times hawk watchers can station themselves at spots just south of Hoopersville, in the center of Middle Hooper Island, around Ferry Point at the southern end of Upper Hooper Island, just west of Fishing Creek, or north of Honga just before the Hooper Island Road crosses onto Upper Hooper Island. *Warning:* The residents of Hooper Island have a long and sometimes fierce tradition of independence and have been known to shoot at strangers who are trespassing. They also have a tradition of shooting and eating migrating hawks and other birds! Let the hawk watcher beware!

**Access:** From Cambridge follow Route 16 south to Church Creek. Then follow Route 335 south to Hooper Island and the villages of Honga, Fishing Creek, and Hoopersville.

**References:** *Bulletin Natural History Society of Maryland,* 1935, 5 (7):36–40; *GBF.*

## Kent Island (near Stevensville)

**Spring Flights:** None.
**Autumn Flights:** Fair.
**Description:** A narrow island extending southward into Chesapeake Bay with largely rural land that is wooded or under cultivation.

**Access:** From Grasonville drive west on U.S. Route 50–301 to the town of Stevensville. Then continue south on Route 8 as far

as possible on Kent Island toward its southern tip. Hawk watching is done from the highway, near the tip, anywhere adjacent to open habitats with good visibility. Do not trespass.
**Reference:** None.

## Roth Rock Fire Tower (near Oakland)

**Spring Flights:** None.
**Autumn Flights:** Good.
**Description:** A fire tower on the crest of Backbone Mountain providing unrestricted views in all directions.
**Access:** From Oakland drive south on U.S. Route 219 to Red House. Then continue east on U.S. Route 50 for 2.5 miles (4 kilometers). Turn south there onto a paved road and continue for 1 mile (1.6 kilometers) to the top of Backbone Mountain. Then turn right and continue for another mile (1.6 kilometers) on a steep, stony road to the fire tower.
**Reference:** GBF.

## Sandy Point State Park (near Annapolis)

**Spring Flights:** Fair.
**Autumn Flights:** Fair.
**Description:** A point extending into Chesapeake Bay.
**Access:** From Annapolis drive northeast on U.S. Route 50 for about 7 miles (11.2 kilometers) to the park, which is located at the western end of the Chesapeake Bay Bridge. Enter the park and ask at the headquarters where the best spots are located for hawk watching.
**References:** *American Birds,* 1976, 30 (1):48; GBF.

## Washington Monument State Park (near Boonsboro)

**Spring Flights:** None.
**Autumn Flights:** Good.
**Description:** The roof of a stone tower in the park.
**Access:** From Boonsboro follow alternate (old) Route 40 to the top of South Mountain. Then turn left onto a road opposite an inn and continue for a mile (1.6 kilometers) to Washington Monument State Park. Enter the park and drive to a parking lot near the stone tower. Walk to the tower via a trail and climb to the top. Observe from there. The park sometimes is called Monument Knob State Park.
**References:** *Atlantic Naturalist,* 1951, 6:166–68; 1966, 21:161–68; AHF; GEHW.

*Observation tower, Washington Monument State Park, Md.*

# Massachusetts

## Blueberry Hill (near Granville)

**Spring Flights:** Poor.
**Autumn Flights:** Excellent.
**Description:** The summit of a hill, known locally as Blueberry Hill, from which migrating hawks are observed.
**Access:** From Westfield drive south on U.S. Route 202 to the junction with State Route 57 near Southwick. Turn west onto Route 57 and continue through Granville to North Lane #2 (a right turn about 3 miles or 4.8 kilometers west of Granville). Turn right (north) onto North Lane #2 and continue for about a mile (1.6 kilometers) to Blueberry Hill on your right. Park at the bottom of the hill. Then walk about 0.25 mile (0.4 kilometer) to the summit from which hawk watching is done.
**References:** *NHMA,* 1976, 1 (2):5; *Bird Observer of Eastern Massachusetts,* 1977, 5 (4):107–11.

# Fisher Hill (in Westhampton)

**Spring Flights:** Poor.
**Autumn Flights:** Good.
**Description:** The exposed top of a hill, at an elevation of 1,309 feet (393 meters), providing an unrestricted view in all directions.
**Access:** At the junction of Routes 9 and 66 in Northampton, drive west on Route 66 for 10.4 miles (16.6 kilometers) to a house on the right side of the highway. On the left, just beyond the house, is an unpaved road. Park near that road and walk up it about 0.25 mile (0.4 kilometer) to the exposed summit from which hawk watching is done.
**Reference:** *NHMA,* 1976, 1 (2):5.

# Martha's Vineyard

**Spring Flights:** None.
**Autumn Flights:** Poor.
**Description:** The shoreline along the southeastern end of Chappaquiddick Island and the entire southern shore of Martha's Vineyard as far as Squibnocket Point and Zacks Cliffs serve as a migration route for limited numbers of Peregrine Falcons in autumn.
**Access:** Various roads on the island pass within close proximity to portions of the shorelines previously mentioned. Some walking and searching for favorable observation spots will be necessary. Most accommodations on the island are available by reservation only.
**References:** *AHF; GEHW.*

# Mount Everett State Reservation (near South Egremont)

**Spring Flights:** Information unavailable.
**Autumn Flights:** Good.
**Description:** An exposed summit of the mountain from which hawk watchers may view migrating hawks.
**Access:** From South Egremont drive west on Routes 23 and 41 following signs pointing toward Jug End Resort. At the point a short distance from South Egremont where the two routes separate, follow Route 41 a little more, then turn right (Route 41 turns left) onto another road marked by a sign pointing to Mount Everett and Jug End Resort. Continue on this road to the first crossroad, then drive straight ahead, uphill, for 2.8 miles (4.4 kilometers) to a fork. Follow the left fork in the road (a sign there points to Bash Bish Falls and Copake Falls, N.Y.) for 3 miles (4.8 kilometers) to the entrance to Mount Everett State Reservation on the left. Drive to the parking lot near the summit of the mountain, and park. Then walk to the top of the mountain from which hawk watching can be enjoyed.
**Reference:** *JHMA,* 1975, 1 (1):8.

*Upridge view from Goat Peak, Mount Tom State Reservation, Mass.*

## Mount Tom State Reservation (near Holyoke)

**Spring Flights:** Poor.
**Autumn Flights:** Good.
**Description:** Observations are made from an open steel tower on the summit of Goat Peak within the reservation.
**Access:** From Interstate 91 take the East Hampton exit and follow Route 141 north for 2.3 miles (3.6 kilometers) to the reservation entrance. Turn right and continue 1.5 miles (2.4 kilometers) into the reserve to the Goat Peak parking lot. Then walk along a well-used trail to the Goat Peak observation tower.
**References:** *Bulletin Massachusetts Audubon Society,* 1937, 21:5–8; *AHF; GEHW.*

## Mount Wachusett State Reservation (at Princeton)

**Spring Flights:** Information unavailable.
**Autumn Flights:** Excellent.
**Description:** A 2,006-foot-high (602 meters) mountain providing views of Boston to the east and the Berkshire Mountains to the west. No single spot provides good views in all directions, but the lookout facing Leominister seems to be the best for hawk watching followed by the view to the right of the fire tower (especially good for accipiters). Broad-winged Hawks are the

most commonly seen raptors followed by Sharp-shinned Hawks then lesser numbers of other species.

**Access:** From Boston drive west on Route 2 to the junction with Route 140 in Westminster. Turn south onto Route 140 and continue to Wachusett Lake. At that point turn right onto Mile Hill Road and follow the signs to the Mt. Wachusett Ski Area. Approximately 0.5 mile (0.8 kilometer) past the ski area you will arrive at the entrance to the reservation on the right. Enter and drive to the summit of the mountain following the reserve's paved road. This road usually is open by 8:00 A.M., although it is marked as opening at 10:00 A.M., and remains open until dusk. After 30 October the road is closed for the season. Park at the top of the mountain and walk to the hawk-watching spots previously described.

**Reference:** *Bird Observer of Eastern Massachusetts,* 1977, 5 (4):107–11.

## Parker River National Wildlife Refuge (on Plum Island)

**Spring Flights:** Fair.
**Autumn Flights:** Information unavailable.
**Description:** A barrier beach island the southern half of which forms part of the Parker River National Wildlife Refuge. Most migrating hawks can be seen from any dune on the ocean side of the northern half of the refuge, or from the main parking lot (Lot No. 1). American Kestrels and Sharp-shinned Hawks are the most commonly observed species, but other species including some Merlins also can be expected.

**Access:** From Boston follow U.S. Route 1 north for about 35 miles (56 kilometers) to Hanover Street in Newbury. Turn right onto Hanover Street (which becomes Rolfe's Lane at the first set of traffic lights) and drive to the harbor. Turn right there onto Water Street which becomes the Plum Island Turnpike and follow it to Plum Island. Once on the island turn at the first right and follow that road to the refuge entrance. Enter and continue driving to the main parking lot or another spot you select to watch migrating hawks.

**Reference:** *Bird Observer of Eastern Massachusetts,* 1978, 6 (1):10–22.

## Province Lands State Reservation (near Provincetown)

**Spring Flights:** Fair.
**Autumn Flights:** Information unavailable.
**Description:** The observation deck of the visitors' center from which falcons can be seen over the outer beach, or the summit

of High Dune from which clear views in all directions are enjoyed.

**Access:** In Provincetown, at the outer tip of Cape Cod, follow U.S. Route 6 to Race Point Road. Turn left onto Race Point Road and continue driving to the visitors' center from which hawk watching can be done. Alternatively stop at the Beech Forest parking lot (the first on the left) after turning from Route 6 onto Race Point Road. Park there, then walk on the trail to the south of Wood Duck Pond (to your left when facing the pond from the parking lot) to a section of split rail fence on the south side of the trail. Turn south along the sandy trail. Then pass through scrub pine to the summit of High Dune (the highest point in the area) from which observations are made.

**Reference:** *Bird Observer of Eastern Massachusetts,* 1978, 6 (2):40–47.


## Quabbin Reservoir (near Belchertown)

**Spring Flights:** Information unavailable.
**Autumn Flights:** Good.
**Description:** A lookout tower with nearby picnic and parking facilities.
**Access:** From Ware drive west on State Route 9 for 7.25 miles (11.6 kilometers) to the Winsor Dam entrance to Quabbin Reservoir. Enter, then drive to the parking lot near the observation tower. After parking walk to the tower or open areas nearby and observe from there.
**Reference:** *JHMA,* 1975, 1 (1):8.


## Round Top Hill (in Athol)

**Spring Flights:** Poor.
**Autumn Flights:** Good.
**Description:** An exposed summit of a 1,207-foot-high (362 meters) hill from which unrestricted observations in all directions are possible. Hawk watching is done from a picnic table at the highest point on the hill.

**Access:** From the center of Athol drive east on Main Street until Athol Memorial Hospital appears on the right. At the sign "Athol Conservation Area" turn left onto Bearsden Road and follow it north for about a mile (1.6 kilometers) to a fork in the road. Take the right fork, following the "Athol Conservation Area" signs to a point where the road is unpaved. Park here at a suitable spot. Then walk along the road to a sign on the right reading "Round Top Path." Follow this well-marked trail for about 0.5 mile (0.8 kilometer) to the summit of the exposed hill and the picnic table from which hawk-watching is done.
**Reference:** *NHMA,* 1976, 1 (2):5.

# Michigan

## Brockway Mountain (near Copper Harbor)

**Spring Flights:** Good.
**Autumn Flights:** Information unavailable.
**Description:** The exposed, treeless summit of an east-to-west ridge at the northern end of the Keweenaw Peninsula.
**Access:** From the twin cities of Hancock and Houghton, drive north on U.S. Route 41 for about 24 miles (38.4 kilometers) to Phoenix (a "ghost town" of about a dozen houses along the highway). At Phoenix turn left onto State Route 26 and continue for about 2 miles (3.2 kilometers) to the village of Eagle River. Remain on Route 26 for another 8 miles (12.8 kilometers) to Eagle Harbor, where the road makes a sharp right followed by a sharp left, and continue for 4.5 miles (7.2 kilometers) to the point in which the highway crosses a small stone bridge over the Silver River. Route 26 bears left here and the Brockway Mountain Drive bears right. Follow the Brockway Mountain Drive for about 5 miles (8 kilometers) to the top of the mountain. At times, early in the season, the road may not yet be clear of snow and it is sometimes necessary to walk for several miles (kilometers) to the summit. Be prepared for very cold, windy weather on top of the mountain.
**Reference:** *Birding*, 1977, 9 (2):79–80.

## Port Huron

**Spring Flights:** Information unavailable.
**Autumn Flights:** Fair.
**Description:** Complete details are unavailable on this site, but exposed areas near either end of the bridge linking Port Huron with Sarnia, Ontario, would probably allow persons to observe migrating hawks passing over or below the bridge as sometimes happens.
**Access:** In Port Huron, or Sarnia, Ontario, drive to a suitable exposed area near either end of the bridge from which a clear view of the bridge and adjacent areas is obtained. Observe from there.
**References:** *Audubon Magazine*, 1962, 64 (1):45; *AHF*.

## Straits of Mackinac (near Mackinaw City)

**Spring Flights:** Good.
**Autumn Flights:** Fair.
**Description:** Areas with exposed views west of Mackinaw City along Wilderness Park Drive.
**Access:** From the Lower Peninsula drive north on Interstate 75 to the last exit from the Interstate before the Mackinac Bridge. Take

this exit onto Wilderness Park Drive and travel west for 1 to 2 miles (1.6 to 3.2 kilometers) from the city limits at which area good hawk watching is possible.

**References:** *Jack-Pine Warbler,* 1965, 43:79–83; *GEHW; GBF.*

## Whitefish Point

**Spring Flights:** Good.
**Autumn Flights:** Fair.
**Description:** A parking lot near the lighthouse, the road leading to the point, or the dunes west of the road near the shoreline.
**Access:** From the Lower Peninsula cross the Straits of Mackinac on Interstate 75 and continue northward to the junction of Route 123. Turn onto Route 123 and continue north to Paradise. Then follow an unnumbered road north for about 12 miles (19.2 kilometers) to Whitefish Point.
**References:** *Jack-Pine Warbler,* 1965, 43:79–83; *GEHW.*

# Minnesota

## Hawk Ridge Nature Reserve (in Duluth)

**Spring Flights:** Fair.
**Autumn Flights:** Excellent.
**Description:** Bluffs rising 600 to 800 feet above the shoreline of Lake Superior in Duluth. The most important spot, the Skyline Boulevard lookout, is the shoulder of a gravel road (Skyline Parkway).
**Access:** In Duluth drive east on London Road to 47th Avenue East. Turn uphill, continue for a mile (1.6 kilometers) to Glenwood Street. Turn left and continue 0.8 mile (1.3 kilometers) to Skyline Parkway. Turn sharply to the right onto this unpaved road and continue a mile (1.6 kilometers) to the Hawk Ridge Nature Reserve sign. Park along the road and observe near the sign. During the migration season hawk watchers are almost always there.
**References:** *Wilson Bulletin,* 1966:79–87; *AHF; GEHW.*

# New Hampshire

## Little Round Top (near Bristol)

**Spring Flights:** None.
**Autumn Flights:** Good.
**Description:** An exposed summit of a hill with good views in all directions except toward the southwest.

**Access:** From the center of Bristol drive south on Route 3A to a firehouse in the middle of a fork in the road near the edge of town. Follow the right fork up a hill, then turn right at the next fork. Follow this road as far as possible, ignoring all roads which turn sharply right, to the Slim Baker Conservation Area and Day Camp. Park near the main building. Then walk along a trail or old road to the lookout on the northeast corner of the hilltop—about a ten-minute walk.

**References:** *AHE; GEHW.*

## Pack Monadnock Mountain (near Peterborough)

**Spring Flights:** Information unavailable.

**Autumn Flights:** Fair.

**Description:** A mountain summit providing exposed views of migrating hawks.

**Access:** From Peterborough drive east on State Route 101 for a few miles (kilometers) to the Miller State Park entrance. Enter the park and drive (toll) to the summit (South Pack) of Pack Monadnock Mountain from which hawk watching is done.

**Reference:** *Bird Observer of Eastern Massachusetts,* 1977, 5 (4):107–11.

## Peaked Hill (near New Hampton)

**Spring Flights:** Good.

**Autumn Flights:** Poor.

*Skyline Boulevard Lookout, Hawk Ridge Nature Reserve, Duluth, Minn.*

**Description:** A vista from a road overlooking large fields.

**Access:** From Interstate 93 near Bristol take Exit 23 and follow Route 104 toward Bristol. Cross a bridge and at the next right turn onto River Road. Drive to the fork, keep right, then continue to and take the next *sharp* left turn. Drive up the hill past the last farmhouse and stop at a cattle gate on the left. Remain on the side of the road at this spot and look over the fields on both sides of the road for migrating hawks.

**Reference:** *GEHW.*

## Pitcher Mountain (near Keene)

**Spring Flights:** Information unavailable.

**Autumn Flights:** Fair.

**Description:** A broad, treeless mountain summit (elevation 2,153 feet or 646 meters) providing a 360-degree view. A fire tower is located on the summit.

**Access:** From Keene, in southern New Hampshire, drive north on Route 10 to the junction with Route 9, then continue north on Route 9 to the junction with Route 123. Turn left (west) onto Route 123, continue through Stoddard to the entrance of the Pitcher Mountain parking lot marked by a sign along the right side of Route 123 about 2 miles (3.2 kilometers) past Stoddard. Park in the unpaved lot and walk to the summit of the mountain—a 5- or 10-minute hike.

**Reference:** None.

## Uncanoonuc Mountain (near Goffstown)

**Spring Flights:** None.

**Autumn Flights:** Good.

**Description:** A parking lot with visibility restricted by trees, or a fire tower if permission can be secured to use it.

**Access:** From Main Street in Goffstown, drive on Mountain Road keeping left around two sharp curves at two intersections. Turn left again onto Mountain Summit Road, following it to the top of the mountain. Park near the fire tower.

**References:** *AHE; GEHW.*

# New Jersey

## Bearfort Mountain (in West Milford Township)

**Spring Flights:** Fair.

**Autumn Flights:** Fair.

**Description:** A rocky outcropping near the base of the Bearfort Fire Tower or occasionally the fire tower itself.

**Access:** From Newfoundland drive north on Route 23 for a mile (1.6 kilometers), then turn right onto Union Valley Road. Continue for 5 miles (8 kilometers) to Stephens Road. Then left onto Stephens Road and drive for 0.7 mile (1.1 kilometers) to a foot path on the left. Park about 150 feet (45 meters) beyond the path, then return and follow the path for about 0.5 mile (0.8 kilometer). The lookout rocks are located off the right side of the trail near the fire tower but are partly hidden by vegetation although they are connected to the main trail by a smaller trail extending for a short distance and becoming obscure.

**References:** *Urner Field Observer,* 1970:9–21; 1971:11–17; *AHF; GEHW.*

## Cape May Point

**Spring Flights:** None.
**Autumn Flights:** Excellent.
**Description:** A parking lot beside the lighthouse, exposed areas in front of the lighthouse, or abandoned concrete bunkers along the shoreline a short distance ahead of the lighthouse. Occasionally other areas are productive and their location is determined by watching the flight paths of the hawks on any particular day.
**Access:** Drive south on the Garden State Parkway first to Cape May then to Cape May Point. Head toward the lighthouse and

*Cape May Point, N.J.*

park in the area beside it. Remain there, walk in front of the lighthouse, or follow the park road to the beach where the bunkers are located.

**References:** *Auk,* 1936:393–404; *Bird Studies at Old Cape May* (Dover Publications, 1965); *New Jersey Audubon,* 1977, 3 (7 and 8):114–24.

## Catfish Fire Tower (near Blairstown)

**Spring Flights:** Fair.
**Autumn Flights:** Good.
**Description:** A fire tower placed in a clearing on a forested spur of the Kittatinny Ridge.
**Access:** From Blairstown drive north for several miles (kilometers) on the Blairstown to Millbrook Road to the point where the Appalachian Trail crosses the highway. This is about 2 miles (3.2 kilometers) southwest of Millbrook. Drive southwest along the unpaved road (also the trail) as far as possible and park. Continue walking west along the Appalachian Trail about 1.5 miles (2.4 kilometers) to the fire tower. Other trails cross this area but only the Appalachian Trail is marked with white blazes.
**References:** *New Jersey Nature News,* 1972, 27 (1):19–21; *AHF; GEHW.*

## Greenbrook Sanctuary (near Tenafly)

**Spring Flights:** Information unavailable.
**Autumn Flights:** Excellent.
**Description:** A parking lot near the entrance to the sanctuary, or the edge of the pond in the middle of the sanctuary.
**Access:** From Clinton Avenue (the main east to west street) in Tenafly drive east on Clinton Avenue to State Route 9W (a T intersection). Turn left (north) onto Route 9W and drive about 0.5 mile (0.8 kilometer) to the first road leading to the right (the sanctuary entrance). Turn right and proceed about 300 feet (90 meters) to the gate. Enter after meeting the sanctuary naturalist (by prior arrangement only through the Palisades Nature Association, P.O. Box 155, Alpine, N.J. 07620) and continue to the lookouts previously described. Watch from either of those spots.
**Reference:** *NHMA,* 1977, 2 (2):13.

## Higbee Beach (near Cape May Point)

**Spring Flights:** Information unavailable.
**Autumn Flights:** Good to excellent.
**Description:** On some days with prevailing northwest winds hawks shift their flight lines from the tip of Cape May Point and migrate northward along the New Jersey side of Delaware Bay. Under such conditions one of the best hawk lookouts is located

along Higbee Beach north of Cape May Point. One can sit or stand on the dunes behind the beach or along the shore and watch the migrating hawks pass by. Frequently large numbers of songbirds also appear here under similar weather conditions.

**Access:** From the town of Cape May at the southern terminus of the Garden State Parkway, drive through the town and follow Sunset Boulevard toward Cape May Point for about 2 miles (3.2 kilometers). Then turn right (north) onto Bayshore Road and continue for 1.8 miles (2.8 kilometers) to Higbee Beach Road (the second paved road, marked with a dead-end sign). Turn left (west) onto Higbee Beach Road and continue to the end of the pavement. Park, then walk along an unpaved road through a wooded area to the nearby beach from which migrating hawks and other birds can be observed at various locations.

**References:** *Auk,* 1936:393–404; *Bird Studies at Old Cape May* (Dover Publications, 1965); *GBF.*

## High Point State Park

**Spring Flights:** Information unavailable.
**Autumn Flights:** Fair.
**Description:** An exposed ridge crest with a huge monument. Observe from the vicinity of the base of the monument.
**Access:** In extreme northwestern New Jersey. From Sussex drive north on Route 23 for about 10 miles (16 kilometers) into High Point State Park. Then follow marked park roads to the monument. Alternatively from Interstate 84 at Port Jervis, New York, drive south on Route 23 to the park.
**Reference:** *Annotated List of Birds of High Point State Park and Stokes State Forest* (Dryden Kuser, 1962).

## Island Beach State Park (near Seaside Heights)

**Spring Flights:** Information unavailable.
**Autumn Flights:** Poor.
**Description:** An undisturbed barrier beach island along which considerable numbers of migrating falcons (especially Peregrines and Merlins) as well as limited numbers of other hawks appear. Birds are seen from the ocean or bay side of the island.
**Access:** From Toms River drive east on Route 37 to Seaside Heights. Turn right and follow the island's main road south for a few miles to the Island Beach State Park entrance. A small entrance fee is charged. After entering the park continue south on the main park road to the headquarters. Stop there and secure additional information on locations where hawk watching is permitted. Not all sections of the park are open to public use. *Warning:* Do not walk on dunes or fragile dune vegetation! There are severe penalties for doing so.
**Reference:** *NHMA,* 1978, 3 (2):10–12.

## Montclair Hawk Lookout Sanctuary

**Spring Flights:** None.
**Autumn Flights:** Excellent.
**Description:** An exposed field overlooking a cliff and quarry.

*Montclair Hawk Lookout Sanctuary, N.J.*

**Access:** From Exit 151 of the Garden State Parkway near Montclair drive west on Watchung Avenue for about 2 miles (3.2 kilometers), then turn right onto Upper Mountain Avenue. Remain on this street for about 0.75 mile (1.2 kilometers), then turn left onto Bradford Avenue. Drive ahead on Bradford Avenue for about 0.25 mile (0.4 kilometer) to Edgecliff Road (the second street on the right). Continue to the top of the hill and just before reaching Crestmont Road park in a small, unmarked parking lot beside the road. Walk east to the lookout on a trail which is entered on the south side of the road.
**References:** *AHF; GEHW.*

## Raccoon Ridge (near Blairstown)

**Spring Flights:** Fair.
**Autumn Flights:** Excellent.
**Description:** Two exposed ridge crests on top of the Kittatinny Ridge.
**Access:** From Blairstown drive west on Route 94 for several miles to an ice-cream stand and a sign pointing to the Yards

Creek Pump Storage Station. Drive to the gate of the station, secure permission to enter from the guard on duty, and continue to a small picnic area. Park there and walk uphill on a paved road until a spot is reached where powerlines meet the road. Leave the road and walk north along the obvious powerline cut, cross two small streams, and climb the south slope of the ridge. The last part of this climb is extremely steep and involves vigorous effort. Once on top of the ridge walk eastward along the Appalachian Trail for a few hundred feet (meters) to an exposed area (the Upper Lookout) identified by several small steel remnants from an old fire tower. Alternatively after crossing the second stream and beginning to climb the south slope of the ridge, follow an old log road leading to the right of the powerline cut. Continue on this road uphill to the top of the mountain. This brings you to the Lower Lookout. To visit the Upper Lookout walk west on the Appalachian Trail for about 0.25 mile (0.4 kilometer) to the spot previously mentioned. Either lookout is suitable for hawk watching.

**References:** *New Jersey Nature News,* 1972, 27 (1):22–28; *AHF; GEBW.*

F.T.

*North-northeast view from Raccoon Ridge, N.J.*

## Rifle Camp Park Lookout (near Clifton)

**Spring Flights:** Information unavailable.
**Autumn Flights:** Excellent.
**Description:** The lawn of a nature center in Rifle Camp Park from which hawk watchers have unrestricted views from the northeast to the southwest, and slightly restricted views in other directions. The park is located on top of the Watchung Mountains.
**Access:** From Exit 154 of the Garden State Parkway near Clifton, drive west on U.S. Route 46 for about 3 miles (4.8 kilometers) to

the Great Notch Exit which leads off Route 46 onto Rifle Camp Road. Drive north on Rifle Camp Road for about 2 miles (3.2 kilometers) to the Rifle Camp Park entrance. Enter the park and drive to the nature center building where hawk watching is done from the lawn outside the building. Additional information, water, and restroom facilities are available at the nature center. **Reference:** *NHMA,* 1977, 2 (2):13.

## Sandy Hook (near Highlands)

**Spring Flights:** Good.
**Autumn Flights:** Information unavailable.
**Description:** Exposed areas along the eastern side of the park or other open areas near the heliport parking area.
**Access:** From Exit 117 of the Garden State Parkway near Matawan, drive east on Route 36 through Highlands, across the Highlands bridge, to the entrance to Sandy Hook and the Gateway National Recreation Area. Enter the park and drive north to the ranger station / gatehouse. On request, the ranger will issue to you a birder's map, rules, and an automobile pass. Drive north through the park (following the map) to the parking area marked heliport parking area. Park there and observe from open areas near the helicopter landing site (helofield) or walk eastward to Battery Gunnison on the eastern side of the peninsula and observe from open areas about 500 feet (150 meters) south of Battery Gunnison. Additional information may be obtained by writing to Gateway National Recreation Area, Sandy Hook Unit, P.O. Box 437, Highlands, N.J. 07732.
**Reference:** *NHMA,* 1978, 3 (1):4–6.

## Scott's Mountain Hawk Lookout (near Phillipsburg)

**Spring Flights:** Poor.
**Autumn Flights:** Fair.
**Description:** A roadside overlooking open agricultural land. Birds approach from the north-northwest and pass overhead.
**Access:** From Phillipsburg drive east on Route 22 to Route 57, then east on Route 57 to the junction with Route 519. Turn left onto Route 519 and follow it north to Scott's Mountain. At the junction of Fox Farm Road turn right onto that road and follow it eastward to a point where several radio towers are visible north of the road. Observe from that area.
**Reference:** None.

## Skyline Ridge (near Oakland)

**Spring Flights:** Information unavailable.
**Autumn Flights:** Excellent.

**Description:** An outcropping of rocks on a ridge from which observers look over the Wanque Valley toward the west, New York State toward the northwest, and High Mountain and New York City toward the southeast. Trees block visibility toward the northeast.

**Access:** From Oakland drive west on State Route 208 to the end of the highway in Oakland. At the point where Route 208 ends, continue straight onto West Oakland Avenue. Cross the Ramapo River and continue about an eighth of a mile (0.1 kilometer) to a T in the road. Turn right at the T onto Skyline Drive and continue on this road to a point where it begins to descend the western slope of the ridge. Look for an open area (a gas pipeline) and a "Leaving Oakland" sign. Park at a suitable spot near this sign and pipeline, or continue a short distance down the road and park on the left side across from a "Ringwood" sign. From here walk down Skyline Drive to a Lion's Club sign. Then go left over a guard rail and hike up a short, steep incline to the lookout rocks from which observations are made.

**Reference:** *NHMA,* 1977, 2 (2):13.

## Sunrise Mountain

**Spring Flights:** Information unavailable
**Autumn Flights:** Good.

**Description:** An exposed area on the Appalachian Trail part of which is covered by an open-sided shelter. Unrestricted views are secured toward the south and northwest, but the view northeast is slightly restricted.

**Access:** From Newton drive north on Route 206 to Stokes State Forest, then follow directional signs to the Sunrise Mountain overlook. Park in the parking lot and walk along a well-used trail to the open-sided shelter over the Appalachian Trail. The walk requires about five minutes.

**References:** *AHF; GEHW.*

## Tuckerton Meadows (near Tuckerton)

**Spring Flights:** Information unavailable.
**Autumn Flights:** Poor.

**Description:** Extensive salt marshes, mud flats, and brackish pools bisected by a narrow road.

**Access:** From Tuckerton drive west on U.S. Route 9 to Great Bay Boulevard, then turn south onto the boulevard and follow it for several miles (kilometers) to its terminus overlooking Little Egg Inlet. The road becomes very narrow at places, crosses several small bridges, and is an excellent birding spot. Migrating Peregrine Falcons, Merlins, and other raptors can be expected to appear in small numbers almost anywhere along the road or

over the adjacent salt meadows. However, the area is not out-standing as a hawk-migration observation area.
**Reference:** *GBF.*


# New Mexico

## Sierra Grande (in Union County)

**Spring Flights:** Information unavailable.
**Autumn Flights:** Fair.
**Description:** An exposed area toward the top of a massive vol-canic shield mountain rising from the surrounding prairie to an elevation of 8,732 feet (2,620 meters). The best hawk-watching spot is on the north face of the mountain at about treeline (ca. 7,500 feet or 2,250 meters).
**Access:** From Des Moines in extreme northeastern New Mexico, drive west on U.S. Route 64–87 for about 2 miles (3.2 kilome-ters) to an unpaved road leading toward a windmill with a stone tank beside it. Turn and follow this road, which becomes very rough, south toward the crest of the mountain. To continue it is necessary to contact the cattle inspector in Des Moines concern-ing entry into the area through a locked gate.
**Reference:** *New Mexico Ornithological Society Bulletin,* 1977, 5 (1):7.


# New York

## Bear Mountain State Park (near Nyack)

**Spring Flights:** Information unavailable.
**Autumn Flights:** Good.
**Description:** An overlook, just beyond the main parking area on top of Bear Mountain, from which unobstructed views are avail-able in all directions.
**Access:** From Nyack drive west on Interstate Routes 287 and 87 to the Palisades Interstate Parkway, then drive north on the park-way to the Bear Mountain Bridge traffic circle. Stop at the main complex of buildings just off (west) the bridge circle to inform the park superintendent and/or the park police that you will be spending the day on top of Bear Mountain and will drive there via Perkins Memorial Drive. After leaving the park headquarters drive 1.5 miles (2.4 kilometers) west on Seven Lakes Drive (the road in front of the headquarters building) to a sign pointing to Perkins Memorial Drive. Turn right onto the drive, pass through an open gate, and continue to the top of the mountain. Park in the main parking area and walk to the lookout previously de-

scribed. Observe from there. Persons approaching on the Palisades Interstate Parkway can leave the parkway at Exit 15 to reach Perkins Memorial Drive, but it is still necessary to drive 2.3 miles (3.6 kilometers) to the park headquarters at the bridge circle before returning to the road leading to the top of the mountain.
**Reference:** None.

## Bonticou Crag (near New Paltz)

**Spring Flights:** Fair.
**Autumn Flights:** Information unavailable.
**Description:** The summit of a bald knob with good views toward the east and south but somewhat restricted views toward the southwest and northwest.
**Access:** From Exit 18 (New Paltz) of the New York State Thruway drive west on Route 299 (Main Street) to the Wallkill River Bridge. Cross the bridge and turn right at the first turn after the bridge. Then turn left at the first left turn and follow the signs to Lake Mohonk. At the top of the mountain (about 4 miles or 6.4 kilometers from the bridge) turn into the Lake Mohonk Mountain House gatehouse and park. Secure a grounds pass (day fee $3.00), then walk from the gatehouse northeast on Bonticou Road for 1.5 miles (2.4 kilometers) to the yellow-marked trail at the foot of Bonticou Crag. Follow the yellow markings to the crag which is about 200 feet (60 meters) high and consists of very steep boulders. The climb to the top requires hands and feet plus rubber-soled shoes. Persons not in good physical condition should not attempt the climb. Once on top of the crag observe from there.
**Reference:** *NHMA*, 1978, 3 (1):9.

## Braddock Bay State Park (Greece)

**Spring Flights:** Excellent.
**Autumn Flights:** None.
**Description:** The parking lot of the park known locally among hawk watchers as Hawk Lookout.
**Access:** From the Lake Ontario State Parkway on the north side of Rochester, drive west for several miles to the East Manitou Road exit ramp. Leave the parkway there and turn right at the stop sign, then drive about 500 feet (150 meters) to the Braddock Bay State Park entrance. Enter the park and drive another 0.4 mile (0.6 kilometer) to the parking lot from which hawk watching is done.
**Reference:** *California Condor*, 1972, 7 (5):9–10; *GEHW*.

## Cattaraugus Creek (near Irving)

**Spring Flights:** Good.
**Autumn Flights:** None.
**Description:** The mouth of Cattaraugus Creek (for flights of accipiters) or higher ground nearby (for flights of Broad-winged Hawks).
**Access:** From Exit 58 on Interstate 90 near Irving turn right onto State Route 5. Cross Cattaraugus Creek, then turn left and continue to an underpass beyond which you should turn left again following the road to the northeast side of the mouth of the creek from which large flights of migrating Sharp-shinned Hawks are sometimes seen. Alternatively return to State Route 5 and continue west for about a mile (1.6 kilometers), then drive south on Allegheny Road to higher ground near Lake Erie from which flights of Broad-winged Hawks are seen.
**Reference:** *GBF.*

## Derby Hill (near Mexico)

**Spring Flights:** Excellent.
**Autumn Flights:** None.
**Description:** An exposed field on a ridge near the shoreline of Lake Ontario.

*Derby Hill, N.Y.*

**Access:** From Mexico drive north on Route 3 for 4.5 miles (7.2 kilometers) to the junction with Route 104B. Turn west onto Route 104B and continue for 0.5 mile (0.8 kilometer) to the corner of Sage Creek Drive (marked by a barn with twin silos). Turn onto Sage Creek Drive and continue to the end. Park along the road or turn right onto an unpaved road and park at the top of the hill. Walk to the field on the right. This is only about 100 feet (30 meters) from a cliff overlooking Lake Ontario.

**References:** *Kingbird,* 1966, 16 (1):5–16; *Wilson Bulletin,* 1966: 88–110; *GEHW.*

## Fire Island (Robert Moses State Park near Babylon)

**Spring Flights:** None.
**Autumn Flights:** Good.
**Description:** The beach or dunes at Democrat Point at the western end of the island. Alternatively on top of high dunes halfway between the eastern boundary of the park and the Fire Island lighthouse. Any narrow spot along the beach with an unobstructed view across the width of the island is also satisfactory.
**Access:** From Babylon drive east on Route 27A then south on the Robert Moses Causeway across Captree State Park and the Fire Island Inlet into Robert Moses State Park. If parking areas Nos. 4 and 5 are open, park in No. 5 and walk eastward toward the lighthouse. If they are closed, park in area No. 3. To visit Democrat Point, park in area No. 2 and walk to the western end of the island.
**References:** *Kingbird,* 1963, 13 (1):4–12; *AHF; GEHW.*

## Fishers Island

**Spring Flights:** None.
**Autumn Flights:** Fair.
**Description:** The top of Mount Chocomount, about three-quarters of the way down the island, or just to the west of a small bluff near the east end of Beach Pond at Middlefarm Flats about halfway down the island.
**Access:** By the Fishers Island ferryboats (the Mystic Isle or the Olinda) which leave from the vicinity of the old railroad station at the foot of State Street in New London, Connecticut.
**References:** *Auk,* 1922:488–96; *AHF; GEHW.*

## Franklin Mountain (near Oneonta)

**Spring Flights:** Fair.
**Autumn Flights:** Fair.
**Description:** The summit of a hill (elevation 2,120 feet or 636 meters) overlooking the Susquehanna River valley.

**Access:** From the junction of Routes 23 and 28 south of Oneonta, follow the road marked Southside Drive for about 1 mile (1.6 kilometers), then turn right onto an unpaved road marked Swart Hollow. Continue on this road for 1.25 miles (2 kilometers), then make a sharp right turn onto an unmarked and unpaved road continuing up a short, steep incline. Continue for another 0.25 mile (0.4 kilometer) to an iron gate on the right side of the road. Park, climb over the gate, and walk to the top of the small hill on which a telephone micro-reflector is positioned. Observe from the vicinity of the reflector base.

**Reference:** *Kingbird*, 1977, 27:74–79.

## Hook Mountain (near Nyack)

**Spring Flights:** Fair.
**Autumn Flights:** Excellent.
**Description:** An exposed clearing on the summit of a ridge crest.
**Access:** From the New York Thruway drive north on Route 9W (near Nyack) for 2 miles (3.2 kilometers). Park in a "dump" on the right side of the road near the bottom of a hill, or in suitable spots beside the road near the top of the hill. Then walk uphill or downhill from the respective parking area to several telephone cable markers and some blue marks painted on the road. Enter the trail on the right (when walking uphill) and follow the blue trail blazes for a considerable distance to the lookout. The hike'

*Hook Mountain, N.Y.*

requires about 25 minutes and is a very strenuous climb most of the way.

**References:** *California Condor,* 1971, 6 (3):13; 1971, 6 (4):12; 1971, 6 (5):10–12; *AHF; GEHW.*

## Jones Beach

**Spring Flights:** None.
**Autumn Flights:** Fair.
**Description:** An exposed area near the southwest corner of Zach's Bay between the bay and a fishing station.
**Access:** From the Long Island Expressway or the Southern State Parkway drive south on the Meadowbrook State Parkway into Jones Beach State Park. Within the park drive east on Ocean Parkway to parking field No. 4 or 6 (5 is closed during autumn), then walk to the Zach's Bay area where hawk watching is done.
**References:** *Kingbird,* 1958, 8 (2):42–43; 1960, 10 (4):157–59; *AFH; GEHW.*

## Mount Peter (near Greenwood Lake)

**Spring Flights:** None.
**Autumn Flights:** Good.
**Description:** An exposed rocky outcropping and clearing on a ridge crest.
**Access:** From Greenwood Lake drive north on Route 17A for about 2 miles (3.2 kilometers) to the Valley View Restaurant. Park here and walk about 200 feet (60 meters) to the ridge crest behind the restaurant's parking lot. Observe from there.
**References:** *Kingbird,* 1967, 17 (3):129–42; 1969, 19 (4):200–203; *AHF; GEHW.*

## Near Trapps Hawk Lookout (near New Paltz)

**Spring Flights:** Information unavailable.
**Autumn Flights:** Fair.
**Description:** An exposed rocky knob on the crest of the Shawangunk Mountain ridge. There is unlimited visibility toward the east and northwest. The view toward the northeast is along the ridge crest across a small gap.
**Access:** From Exit 18 (New Paltz) of the New York Thruway drive west on Route 299 (Main Street) to the junction with Route 44/55. Turn right and continue for about 1.5 miles (2.4 kilometers) to the Trapps Bridge (the only bridge over the highway). Park near the bridge, pay a nominal entrance fee, and enter the Mohonk Trust Preserve by walking about 200 feet (60 meters) southwest on the carriage road (Trapps Road) to the beginning of the Millbrook Ridge Trail identified by three blue dots on a tree.

Follow the blue marked trail up steep rock slabs for about 700 feet (210 meters) to the ridge crest. The lookout is marked by a bronze "National Ocean Survey" benchmark.

**References:** *AHF; NHMA,* 1976, 2 (2):13.

## Oneida Lookout

**Spring Flights:** None.
**Autumn Flights:** Good.
**Description:** The crest of a lightly traveled road with good views toward the west, north, and east.
**Access:** From the Verona exit of Interstate 90 (Exit 33 of the New York Thruway) drive south on Route 365 to Route 5, then east on Route 5 to Route 26. Turn south onto Route 26 and continue for 6.7 miles (10.7 kilometers) to the intersection of Knoxboro Road. Turn right (west) onto Knoxboro Road and continue for 2.2 miles (3.5 kilometers) uphill to Hatella Road (marked by a small stone block building on the northwest corner). Turn right (north) onto Hatella Road and continue for 1.6 miles (2.5 kilometers), passing the county dump, to a point where the road makes a sharp turn to the west. The lookout is located at the top of the hill. Park along the side of the road.
**References:** *NHMA,* 1976, 1 (2):12–13; *Kingbird,* 1977, 27 (2):82–85.

## Port Jervis Hawk Lookout

**Spring Flights:** Information unavailable.
**Autumn Flights:** Good.
**Description:** A roadside pullover and overlook along the westbound lanes of Interstate 84 about 2 miles (3.2 kilometers) east of Port Jervis. Good views are enjoyed toward the west, north, and northeast. This site should be particularly good on days with prevailing northwest or north winds.
**Access:** From Port Jervis drive east on Interstate 84 to the top of the mountain where several roadside pullover areas will be seen. To reach the overlook used for hawk watching along the westbound lanes it is necessary to drive eastward to the next exit. Leave Interstate 84 there, reverse direction, enter Interstate 84 again heading west, and return to the overlook on top of the mountain. Park and observe there or a few hundred feet (meters) west of the end of the overlook at which point the visibility is better.
**Reference:** *NHMA,* 1977, 2 (2):13.

## Storm King Mountain (near Cornwall-on-Hudson)

**Spring Flights:** Poor.
**Autumn Flights:** Good.

**Description:** An exposed rocky area on the south side of the top of Storm King Mountain overlooking Route 9W. There are unrestricted views in all directions.

**Access:** Park in an unpaved parking lot across from the entrance to the Whitehorse Mountain Hawk lookout. Then hike along a trail (well marked with yellow paint) beginning on the west side of the parking lot and continue on the main trail to the top of the mountain. Observe from the spot previously described. The last half of the trail requires strenuous climbing.

**Reference:** *Enjoying Birds Around New York City* (Houghton Mifflin, 1966).

## Whitehorse Mountain (near Cornwall-on-Hudson)

**Spring Flights:** Poor.

**Autumn Flights:** Excellent.

**Description:** An exposed rocky outcropping providing a circular view from the top of a 1,200-foot-high (360 meters) mountain. Two observation towers are available at the lookout for the use of hawk watchers. Hawk watching is also possible from the ground.

**Access:** From the George Washington Bridge linking New York City with New Jersey, drive north on the Palisades Interstate Parkway to the Bear Mountain Bridge circle, then continue north on Route 9-W for 8.6 miles (13.7 kilometers) to a driveway (marked Paul Jeheber) on the left side of the road where the highway passes over a gap between Whitehorse and Storm King mountains. Persons coming south from Newburgh will drive south on Route 9-W for about 5 miles (8 kilometers) to the driveway on the right side of the road. Park off the road at the entrance to the driveway, or enter and drive a short distance to a house where one may park. Then walk along a well-defined trail (an old wood road) past the front of the house and up the mountainside for about 15 minutes until you reach the lookout. This site is private property and particular care should be taken to avoid littering or otherwise destroying the property. Paul Jeheber, the owner, can provide additional details about hawk watching at Whitehorse Mountain when visitors arrive there.

**Reference:** *Kingbird,* 1976, 26 (3):136–40.

# North Carolina

Although information on hawk flights along the inland mountains of North Carolina is too limited to provide details on suitable hawk lookouts, except for one or two locations, some cursory comments are possible. Various sites along the Blue Ridge Parkway—the area between Little Switzerland, Mount Mitchell, and Thunder Hill—have produced hawk flights in the past.

Other Blue Ridge Parkway sites from which hawk flights have been reported include Blowing Rock, Doughton Park, and Roaring Gap. Table Rock, on the eastern edge of the Blue Ridge, is also used as a hawk lookout at times.

## Bodie Island Lighthouse (near Nags Head)

**Spring Flights:** Information unavailable.
**Autumn Flights:** Fair.
**Description:** The edge of pine woodland around the Bodie Island lighthouse. The spot is a staging area only for migrating accipiters.
**Access:** From Manns Harbor drive east on U.S. Route 64 to Nags Head, then continue about 5 miles (8 kilometers) south from Nags Head to the wooded area around the lighthouse. Observe from any open area around the site.
**Reference:** *Assn. Southeast Biologists Bulletin,* 1978, 25 (2):53–54.

## Buxton Woods (near Buxton)

**Spring Flights:** Information unavailable.
**Autumn Flights:** Fair.
**Description:** The edge of a wooded area located about 0.5 mile (0.8 kilometer) southwest of the Cape Hatteras lighthouse. Most hawks are seen from mid-afternoon to dusk. Accipiters are most common.
**Access:** From Manns Harbor drive east on U.S. Route 64 for a few miles (kilometers) to the junction with State Route 12, then follow Route 12 south to Buxton. The wooded area is located about half a mile (0.8 kilometer) southwest of the nearby lighthouse. Observe from any open area along the ocean side of the site.
**Reference:** *Assn. Southeast Biologists Bulletin,* 1978, 25 (2):53–54.

## Craggy Gardens (north of Oteen)

**Spring Flights:** None.
**Autumn Flights:** Good.
**Description:** "Balds" at the 5,497-foot elevation (1,649 meters) with panoramic views of forested slopes below.
**Access:** From Oteen drive north on the Blue Ridge Parkway for 18 miles (28.8 kilometers) to Craggy Gardens. Observe from the previously mentioned balds.
**Reference:** *GBF.*

# Fort Macon State Park (near Morehead City)

**Spring Flights:** Information unavailable.
**Autumn Flights:** Fair.
**Description:** The top of sand dunes on a barrier beach island providing views over the island and nearby ocean and sound. Accipiters and falcons, including Peregrine Falcons, are seen most frequently. Hawks approach from the north end of the island and often fly only 4 to 6 feet (1.2 to 1.8 meters) above the island; thus observers must remain alert to avoid missing the birds. Late September to mid-October is the best observation period.
**Access:** From Morehead City drive south for a short distance to the park. Continue to the visitors' parking lot, then walk to and climb the highest sand dune southeast of the lot. Observe from there.
**Reference:** *Assn. Southeast Biologists Bulletin,* 1978, 25 (2):53–54.

# Hatteras Island (on the Outer Banks)

**Spring Flights:** Information unavailable.
**Autumn Flights:** Fair.
**Description:** The tops of sand dunes at two narrow sections of a barrier beach island. Many hawks tend to fly only 4 to 6 feet (1.2 to 1.8 meters) above the island, and observers must remain alert or the birds can be overlooked. Late September to mid-October is the best observation period for Ospreys, accipiters, harriers, and falcons (including Peregrine Falcons).
**Access:** From the village of Hatteras drive north on State Route 12 for about 0.5 mile (0.8 kilometer) to a narrow section of the island. Park, climb to the top of a high dune, and observe from there. Alternatively drive south from Hatteras on State Route 12 to the Ocracoke Island Ferry Terminal. Then drive another 0.25 mile (0.4 kilometer) south of the terminal to the end of the paved road. Park, climb to the top of a high dune, and observe from there. Special care must be taken to avoid damaging the vegetation on the dunes.
**Reference:** *Assn. Southeast Biologists Bulletin,* 1978, 25 (2):53–54.

# Pea Island (on the Outer Banks)

**Spring Flights:** Information unavailable.
**Autumn Flights:** Fair.
**Description:** Exposed areas or the tops of sand dunes on a barrier beach island. Late September to mid-October is the best

observation period. Many hawks tend to fly only 4 to 6 feet (1.2 to 1.8 meters) above the island and observers must remain alert or the birds can be overlooked. Mostly accipiters, harriers, and falcons are seen here. Occasionally Peregrine Falcons appear. **Access:** From Manns Harbor drive east on U.S. Route 64 to the junction with State Route 12. Drive south on Route 12 for a few miles (kilometers). Cross the Oregon Inlet Bridge and observe from a point about 0.25 mile (0.4 kilometer) east of the south end of the bridge. Alternatively drive to the headquarters building on Pea Island National Wildlife Refuge somewhat further south on Route 12 and observe from open areas near the headquarters building. A third possible site is reached by driving south on Route 12 to the southern end of the Pea Island National Wildlife Refuge, where one can observe from a narrow portion of the island.
**Reference:** *Assn. Southeast Biologists Bulletin,* 1978, 25 (2):53–54.


# Ohio

## Conneaut

**Spring Flights:** Good.
**Autumn Flights:** None.
**Description:** Open fields on the lake plain near the shoreline of Lake Erie.
**Access:** From Interstate 90 south of Conneaut, take the Conneaut-Andover interchange and drive north on Route 7 into Conneaut (where Route 7 becomes Mill Street). Continue to Lake Road, turn left, and continue west on Lake Road to Parrish Road. Turn left onto Parrish Road and continue to a large white barn on the west side of the street. Permission should be obtained to park near the barn which is on private property.
**Reference:** *GEHW.*


## Lakewood Park (Cleveland)

**Spring Flights:** Good.
**Autumn Flights:** None.
**Description:** A landfill projecting into Lake Erie from which one has a fine view of bluffs toward the east and west.
**Access:** From Interstate 80 (south of Cleveland) drive north on Interstate 71 into the city to the junction with 130 Street. Drive north on 130 Street to Route 10 (Lorain Avenue). Then turn east onto Route 10 and continue to West 117 Street. Turn onto West 117 Street and continue north to Lake Avenue. Turn left (west) onto Lake Avenue and continue to the intersection of Belle Avenue. Turn right into Lakewood Park and drive to the lakefront

landfill extending into the lake from which observations are made.

**References:** *Cleveland Bird Calendar,* 1962, 58 (3):28–33; 1963, 59 (3):28–31; *GEHW.*

## Perkins Beach (Cleveland)

**Spring Flights:** Good.
**Autumn Flights:** None.
**Description:** The top of bluffs overlooking Lake Erie, particularly the top of the rise to the right of West Boulevard.
**Access:** Follow the directions to Lakewood Park as far as Lake Avenue, at which point turn right (east) onto the avenue. Continue to West Boulevard (West 100 Street). Then turn left (north) and continue to the lakefront area formerly known as Perkins Beach. Currently this is the western edge of Edgewater Park.
**References:** *Cleveland Bird Calendar,* 1962, 58 (3):28–33; 1963, 59 (3):28–31; *GEHW.*

## South Bass Island (near Port Clinton)

**Spring Flights:** Fair.
**Autumn Flights:** None.
**Description:** Exposed areas at Lighthouse Point at the extreme southern tip of the island. Most hawk flights occur between 10 April and early May.
**Access:** By ferry from the mainland. The ferryboats leave from the mainland village of Catawba Island (and they dock on South Bass Island a short distance east of Lighthouse Point) or from Port Clinton.
**Reference:** *GBF.*

# Pennsylvania

## Bake Oven Knob (near New Tripoli)

**Spring Flights:** Fair.
**Autumn Flights:** Excellent.
**Description:** Two rocky outcroppings on the crest of the Kittatinny Ridge. The North Lookout (used on westerly and northerly winds) is a small, level area atop a boulder pile. The South Lookout (used on easterly and southerly winds) is an exposed rock outcropping terminated by a 1,000-foot (300 meter) drop to the forested slopes below.
**Access:** At the junction of Routes 309 and 143 at New Tripoli, drive north on Route 309 for 2 miles (3.2 kilometers). Turn right (east) onto a paved road and continue for another 2 miles (3.2 kilometers). Then turn left onto a paved road running between

*South Lookout, Bake Oven Knob, Pa.*

white buildings and a house. Continue on this road for about 0.25 mile (0.4 kilometer). Do not turn when the paved road turns sharply right. Instead drive straight ahead on a gravel road and follow it to the top of the mountain. Park in one of two parking lots, then walk northeast on the Appalachian Trail for about 0.33 mile (0.5 kilometer) to the summit of the knob. Shortly after crossing a large boulder field and climbing a steep incline, look for an old cement foundation beside the trail. The South Lookout is located about 150 feet (45 meters) east of this spot. The North Lookout is reached by continuing to walk northeastward on the Appalachian Trail for about 0.25 mile (0.4 kilometer). After passing a small campsite, walk along the north side of a large boulder pile for about 100 feet (30 meters). Then climb to the top of the boulders to a small, exposed spot at the forward end of the boulder pile. This is the North Lookout.

**References:** *Cassinia,* 1969:11–32; *AHF; GEHW.*


## Bear Rocks (near New Tripoli)

**Spring Flights:** Fair.
**Autumn Flights:** Excellent.
**Description:** A large outcropping of huge boulders on the crest of the Kittatinny Ridge 1.5 miles (2.4 kilometers) southwest of Bake Oven Knob.
**Access:** Drive to the parking lots at Bake Oven Knob. Then walk

southwest (in the opposite direction for visiting the knob) on the Appalachian Trail to a grove of hemlocks and other trees through which the boulder pile can be seen to the right about 200 feet (60 meters) north of the trail. Climb to the top of the boulder pile and select a spot for viewing.

**References:** *AHF; GEHW.*

## Big Rock (near Allentown)

**Spring Flights:** Information unavailable.
**Autumn Flights:** Poor to fair.
**Description:** An outcropping of boulders (elevation 1,038 feet or 311 meters), also known locally as Bauer's Rock, on top of South Mountain just south of Allentown. Excellent views are enjoyed from the top of the rock looking south and southwest, but trees partly or completely block visibility in other directions.
**Access:** From the junction of U.S. Routes 22 and 309 just west of Allentown, drive south on U.S. Route 309 for 7 miles (11.2 kilometers) to the Summit Lawn exit. Leave the main highway here by taking the Summit Lawn off-ramp. Continue to the top of the ramp, then turn left onto the road at the top and drive for about 0.4 mile (0.6 kilometer) to South Pike Avenue. Cross this busy road and continue ahead for another 0.9 mile (1.4 kilome-

*Bear Rocks, Pa.*

ters) to an unpaved parking area at a gate and road leading to several tall communications towers. Park here, off the road. Then walk around the gate and continue uphill on the unpaved road to an area surrounded by a fence. Walk around the left side of the fence on a narrow path. Once in the back of the fenced-in area walk ahead on the trail for a few feet (meters), and Big Rock will be seen ahead of you just off the path. Walk to the rocks, climb to the top (using caution because of broken glass), and observe from there.

**Reference:** None.

## Chickies Rock (near Marietta)

**Spring Flights:** Fair.
**Autumn Flights:** Fair.
**Description:** A 300-foot-high (90 meters) cliff on top of a towering hill overlooking the Susquehanna River. Observers have unrestricted views across the river, upriver, and partly downriver.
**Access:** From Route 30 at Columbia drive north on Route 441 for 1.1 miles (1.7 kilometers) toward Marietta. Park in a large area on the west side of the road just before entering a deep, rocky road cut. Walk west for less than 0.5 mile (0.8 kilometer) following a single pole powerline to a split in the trail. Follow the left fork for another 300 feet (90 meters) to the lookout.
**References:** *GEHW; Hawk Mountain News,* 1978, 50:26.

*Chickies Rock, Pa.*

# Cornwall Fire Tower (near Brickerville)

**Spring Flights:** Poor.
**Autumn Flights:** Good.
**Description:** A fire tower at the 1,200-foot elevation (360 meters) on top of the South Mountain range in Lancaster County.
**Access:** From the junction of Routes 22 and 501 near Bethel, drive south on Route 501 to Route 322 at Brickerville. Turn right (west) onto Route 322 and continue for 4.1 miles (6.5 kilometers) to an unpaved road on the left. Turn left onto the road and follow it for 1.3 miles (2 kilometers) to the fire tower located directly beside the road on the left. Observe from various levels of the tower.
**Reference:** *NHMA,* 1976, 1 (2):13; *Hawk Mountain News,* 1978, 50:26.

# Delaware Water Gap

**Spring Flights:** Information unavailable.
**Autumn Flights:** Good.
**Description:** A series of rocky ledges along the Appalachian Trail just before the trail dips into the gap. One looks across the gap toward the New Jersey side.
**Access:** Drive to Tott's Gap from the north side, following directions provided later in this book for that spot, and continue northeastward for several miles on the unpaved road which runs along the ridge crest to the point where it ends. Park near the base of an old fire tower, then walk northeastward on the Appalachian Trail to the rocky ledges overlooking the gap. The hike from the tower to the ledges requires about five minutes.
**References:** *New Jersey State Museum Science Notes,* 1973, 12:1–3; *AHF; GEHW.*

# Governor Dick Fire Tower (near Mt. Gretna)

**Spring Flights:** Poor.
**Autumn Flights:** Fair.
**Description:** A 65-foot-high (19.5 meters) concrete tower on top of a low mountain providing observers with an unrestricted view in all directions.
**Access:** From Exit 20 (Lebanon-Lancaster) of the Pennsylvania Turnpike (Interstate 76) located north of Manheim, drive north on State Route 72 for 2 miles (3.2 kilometers) to the junction with State Route 117. Turn onto State Route 117 and drive west for 2.5 miles (4 kilometers) to the village of Mt. Gretna. In the village find Pinch Road, located beside a church camp ground, turn left (south) onto it, and drive for 0.6 mile (0.9 kilometer) up the hill to the trail on the left leading to the fire tower. Park, then walk for about 1.1 miles (1.7 kilometers) on the trail to the tower

from which observations are made. Various branch trails lead from the main trail. Therefore, it is important that you generally walk uphill toward the tower rather than on downhill trails. It is necessary to climb hand over hand up steep-rung steps inside the tower to reach the top.

**Reference:** *NHMA,* 1978, 3 (1):9.

## Hawk Mountain Sanctuary (near Kempton)

**Spring Flights:** Fair.
**Autumn Flights:** Excellent.
**Description:** Two rocky outcroppings on the crest of the Kittatinny Ridge. The North Lookout (used on westerly and northerly winds) is atop the main fold of the ridge. The South Lookout (used on easterly and southerly winds) is located about 500 feet (150 meters) behind the entrance gate on a secondary escarpment.

*North Lookout, Hawk Mountain Sanctuary, Pa.*

**Access:** From Allentown or the Northeast Extension of the Pennsylvania Turnpike drive west on Route 22 for a number of miles (kilometers) to the junction of Routes 22 and 143 near Lenhartsville. Turn north onto Route 143 and drive for 4 miles (6.4 kilometers) to a crossroad. Turn left and follow the signs along this paved road to Hawk Mountain. From Hamburg and points toward the west, follow Route 22 (Interstate 78) to the junction of Routes 22 and 61 at Hamburg. Turn north onto Route 61 and continue for several miles (kilometers) to the junction with Route 895. Turn right onto Route 895 and continue another 2 miles (3.2 kilometers) to signs pointing to Drehersville and Hawk Mountain. Turn right again, cross a bridge over a small river, and continue up the mountain to the Hawk Mountain entrance and parking lots. Park in the areas provided and follow the trails to the lookouts. Information can be secured in the headquarters building and information center.

**References:** *Hawks Aloft: The Story of Hawk Mountain* (Dodd, Mead, 1949); *Feathers in the Wind* (Hawk Mountain Sanctuary, 1973).

## Heidelberg Hill Hawk Lookout (near Schnecksville)

**Spring Flights:** Poor (occasionally fair).
**Autumn Flights:** None.
**Description:** A small gravel parking lot on a hilltop overlooking rolling farmland and portions of State Game Land No. 205.
**Access:** From the junction of Routes 22 and 309 northwest of Allentown, drive north on Route 309 to Schnecksville. At the junction of Routes 309 and 873 continue north on Route 309 for 2.8 miles (4.4 kilometers), turn left onto a narrow paved road and continue 0.6 mile (0.9 kilometer) to the top of a hill. Then leave the paved road and continue straight ahead for another 0.3 mile (0.4 kilometer) to a small gravel parking lot on the right. Park in the lot and observe from there toward the southwest.
**Reference:** None.

## Hopewell Fire Tower (near Geigertown)

**Spring Flights:** Information unavailable.
**Autumn Flights:** Good.
**Description:** An 80-foot-high (24 meters) fire tower located on a high knob within French Creek State Park.
**Access:** From the junction of State Routes 724 and 82 at Birdsboro, drive south on Route 82 to Geigertown, then turn left (east) onto another road and drive about 2 miles (3.2 kilometers) into French Creek State Park. Other roads also lead to the park from nearby areas. Persons using the Pennsylvania Turnpike should use Exit 22 (Morgantown). Once at the park drive to the fire tower located toward the southwestern side of the park near a picnic area. A short walk to the tower is necessary.
**Reference:** *Hawk Mountain News,* 1978, 50:26.

## Lake City

**Spring Flights:** Good.
**Autumn Flights:** None.
**Description:** An open field with an unrestricted view to Lake Erie at the rear of the Berkeley Inn Motel.
**Access:** From the intersection of Routes 5 and 18 near Lake City, drive east on Route 5 for about a mile (1.6 kilometers) to the Berkeley Inn Motel. Observe from the area at the rear of the motel. The field over which one looks is private property and open only to foot travel, which must be confined to the unpaved road running down the middle of the field.
**Reference:** *GEHW.*

## Lehigh Furnace Gap

**Spring Flights:** Information unavailable.
**Autumn Flights:** Good.
**Description:** Rocky outcroppings along a powerline right-of-way (on southerly or easterly winds) or rocky outcroppings on the crest of the Kittatinny Ridge (on northerly or westerly winds).
**Access:** At the junction of Routes 309 and 143 at New Tripoli, drive north on Route 309 for 2 miles (3.2 kilometers). Turn right (east) onto a paved road, continue ahead for another 5.2 miles (8.3 kilometers) to a crossroad. Turn left (north) onto another paved road (which eventually becomes gravel) and follow it to the top of the mountain. Park near the communications tower or along the powerline. Then walk along the powerline right-of-way to a high vantage point on the south side of the ridge, or walk east or west on the Appalachian Trail until rocky outcroppings are seen off the trail on one side or the other. Crash through the scrub vegetation to reach these observation sites.
**Reference:** *AHF.*

## Little Gap (near Danielsville)

**Spring Flights:** Information unavailable.
**Autumn Flights:** Excellent.
**Description:** Several outcroppings of boulders on top of the Kittatinny Ridge from which observers can see hawks approaching or flying past the observation rocks.
**Access:** At Danielsville (Northampton County) follow the paved highway north to the top of the Kittatinny Ridge (Blue Mountain). Park in a lot near the top, then continue on foot uphill along the highway to the point where the Appalachian Trail crosses the road. Turn left (west) onto the trail and follow it past a utility pipeline right-of-way (from which migrating hawks can be observed) for about 0.5 mile (0.8 kilometer) until a large boulder pile can be seen off the left (south) side of the trail. Crash

through the scrub vegetation, climb to the top of the boulder pile, and observe from there. Alternatively drive over the top of the mountain on the paved highway, and shortly after starting down the north side turn right onto the property owned by a ski resort. Drive to the ski lodge, park in a suitable spot, and climb the slopes to various high rocky outcroppings on the ridge crest from which migrating hawks also can be seen.

**References:** *AHF; NHMA*, 1976, 1 (2):13; *GEHW.*

## Presque Isle State Park (near Erie)

**Spring Flights:** Fair.
**Autumn Flights:** None.
**Description:** The parking lot at Beach 10 and the shoreline of Lake Erie east of the parking lot. Alternatively the trail starting at the Thompson Bay traffic circle and leading west along Long Ridge.
**Access:** From Interstate 90 drive north on Route 832 to the park entrance near Erie. Secure park maps and other information at the park administration building about a mile (1.6 kilometers) inside the park. Then continue to the lookout areas.
**Reference:** *GEHW.*

## Route 183 (near Strausstown)

**Spring Flights:** Information unavailable.
**Autumn Flights:** Fair.
**Description:** A large, open field with good views toward the north and northeast, but somewhat restricted views in other directions. The best hawk flights are seen here on prevailing north or northwest winds.
**Access:** From the junction of Route 183 and Interstate 78 near Strausstown, drive north on Route 183 past the junction with Route 419 to the top of the Kittatinny Ridge (Blue Mountain). Just before the highway descends the north side of the mountain, turn into an unpaved driveway leading off the left (west) side of the highway into a large field. An old, abandoned cabin stands beside the driveway and highway. Drive into the field and observe from the vicinity of the cabin.
**Reference:** *AHF.*

## Sterrett's Gap

**Spring Flights:** Information unavailable.
**Autumn Flights:** Good.
**Description:** A powerline right-of-way on top of the Kittatinny Ridge, or the same right-of-way beside a paved road on the north slope of the mountain.

**Access:** From the junction of Routes 34 and 944 at Carlisle Springs drive north for several miles (kilometers) on Route 34 to Sterrett's Gap. At the top of the mountain turn right (east) onto Mountain Road (located beside a service station) and continue for 0.3 mile (0.4 kilometer) to the powerline right-of-way. Park at a suitable spot. Then hike uphill along the powerline for a relatively short distance to the ridge crest and observe from there. Alternatively observe from the powerline in the vicinity of the spot where it crosses Mountain Road.

**References:** *Auk,* 1940, 57:247–50; *AHF.*

## Tott's Gap (near Delaware Water Gap)

**Spring Flights:** Information unavailable.

**Autumn Flights:** Fair.

**Description:** A pipeline right-of-way crossing the Kittatinny Ridge and providing a clear view north and south from the ridge crest.

**Access:** In Delaware Water Gap, Pennsylvania, follow Cherry Valley Road to the edge of a golf course, then turn left (west) onto the Poplar Valley Road and continue for several miles (kilometers) to the Tott's Gap Road. Turn left and follow Tott's Gap Road to the top of the mountain. At the top turn left (northeast) and follow the unpaved road for about 0.25 mile (0.4 kilometer) past a communications facility to a radio tower and the pipeline right-of-way. The pipeline is marked by a white steel post beside

*The Pulpit, Tuscarora Mountain, Pa.*

the road. When westerly and northerly winds occur remain near the radio tower and look north over the pipeline cut. On easterly and southerly winds walk south along the pipeline for a few hundred feet to an exposed area and observe from there over the valley south of the ridge.

**References:** *New Jersey State Museum Science Notes,* 1973, 12:1–3; *AHF; GEHW.*

## Tuscarora Mountain (near Chambersburg)

**Spring Flights:** Fair.
**Autumn Flights:** Fair.
**Description:** A flat, exposed area on top of a large pile of rocks known locally as The Pulpit.
**Access:** From Chambersburg drive west on Route 30 toward McConnellsburg. At the top of Tuscarora Mountain park beside an inn and walk along the path (marked by a sign) leading to The Pulpit.
**References:** *AHF; GEHW.*

## Waggoner's Gap (near Carlisle)

**Spring Flights:** Information unavailable.
**Autumn Flights:** Good.
**Description:** A partly exposed boulder pile (used on westerly and northerly winds) on the crest of the Kittatinny Ridge. Alternatively (on easterly and southerly winds) the shoulder of a mountain road.
**Access:** From Carlisle drive north on Route 74 to the top of the Kittatinny Ridge and park near a communication tower. Remain along the roadside near the tower or cross the highway and walk across a parking lot, following a path for about 150 feet (45 meters) to the lookout on the boulder pile. Use caution when climbing over the rocks leading to the boulder pile.
**References:** *Atlantic Naturalist,* 1966, 21:161–68; *AHF; GEHW.*

## West Lake Junior High School (in Erie)

**Spring Flights:** Good.
**Autumn Flights:** None.
**Description:** A grass slope at the rear (northwest corner) of the school. The site overlooks an expanse of land between the school and the shoreline of Lake Erie.
**Access:** The school is located at 4330 West Lake Road (Pennsylvania Route 5A) in Erie. From the junction of State Routes 5A and 832 drive west on Route 5A for about 2 miles (3.2 kilometers) to the school on the north side of the highway.
**Reference:** *GEHW.*

*Waggoner's Gap, Pa.*

# South Carolina

Very limited information is available regarding hawk migrations in South Carolina. It is likely, however, that some flight lines occur along the coast in autumn as well as along the inland mountains.

# Tennessee

### Dunlap Fire Tower (near Chattanooga)

**Spring Flights:** Information unavailable.
**Autumn Flights:** Fair.
**Description:** A fire tower on Walden Ridge where Route 127 crosses the time-zone boundary.
**Access:** From Chattanooga drive north on Route 127 to Walden Ridge. The fire tower is located beside the highway and is readily accessible.
**References:** *AHF; GEHW.*

## Fall Creek Falls State Park (near Spencer)

**Spring Flights:** Information unavailable.
**Autumn Flights:** Fair.
**Description:** A fire tower in the state park, on the Cumberland Plateau.
**Access:** From Pikeville drive northwest on Route 30 for several miles (kilometers) to Fall Creek Falls State Park. Enter the park and continue to the fire tower from which hawk watching is done.
**References:** *Migrant,* 1949, 20 (1):16; *GEHW.*

## Rogersville-Kyles Ford Fire Tower (near Edison)

**Spring Flights:** Information unavailable.
**Autumn Flights:** Good.
**Description:** A fire tower on the crest of Clinch Mountain.
**Access:** From Rogersville drive north on Route 70 to the summit of Clinch Mountain. The fire tower, which can be seen from the road, is located on the ridge east of the highway. Park along the side of the highway, then hike for about ten minutes until the tower is reached.
**References:** *AHF; GEHW.*

# Texas

## Aransas-Copano Bay Area (near Rockport)

**Spring Flights:** Excellent.
**Autumn Flights:** Information unavailable.
**Description:** A suitable, exposed area on the north side of Aransas-Copano bays at the narrowest point near the Copano Bay Bridge. Mid- to late April appears to be a particularly productive hawk watching period.
**Access:** Full details are unavailable on this site, but from Rockport drive north on State Route 35 to the Copano Bay Bridge. Cross the bridge, then seek directions or locate the narrowest north-south point between the bays just west of the Copano causeway from which observations are made.
**Reference:** *NHMA,* 1978, 3 (1):7.

## Bentsen-Rio Grande Valley State Park (near Mission)

**Spring Flights:** Excellent.
**Autumn Flights:** Information unavailable.
**Description:** Open areas on paved roads in the southwestern section of the park adjacent to moist woodlands and dry chaparral.
**Access:** From Mission drive south on Park Road 43 to the park.

More specific directions can be secured in Mission.
**Reference:** *A Birder's Guide to the Rio Grande Valley of Texas* (L & P Photography, 1971).

## Robstown

**Spring Flights:** Information unavailable.
**Autumn Flights:** Excellent.
**Description:** Complete details about this site are unavailable, but presumably one can see impressive flights of migrating hawks from any exposed area along County Route 75.
**Access:** Full details are unavailable. However, from Robstown drive to the junction of U.S. Route 77 and County Route 75. Turn west onto County Route 75 and continue for 4.7 miles (7.5 kilometers) to a point about 1.5 miles (2.4 kilometers) south of the Nueces River. Observe from there.
**Reference:** *NHMA*, 1977, 2 (2):10–11.

## Santa Ana National Wildlife Refuge (near McAllen)

**Spring Flights:** Excellent.
**Autumn Flights:** Information unavailable.
**Description:** The top of a 15-foot-high (4.5 meters) levee providing unrestricted views over the northern portion of the refuge. Large flights of Broad-winged Hawks and Swainson's Hawks (up to 100,000) sometimes occur here in late March and early April. Early morning or evening is the best time to observe the raptors. However, other periods throughout the day should not be overlooked.
**Access:** From McAllen drive south on 10th Street (which becomes Route 336) for about 6 miles (9.6 kilometers) to the junction with U.S. Route 281 (Old Military Road). Turn left (east) onto U.S. Route 281 and continue for another 10 miles (16 kilometers) toward Brownsville. Then look for the refuge sign along the right side of the highway. Turn right and drive for about 0.25 mile (0.4 kilometer) to a levee. Observations are made from a spot on the levee about 100 yards (90 meters) to the right. However, anywhere along the levee is suitable for observing hawk migrations.
**Reference:** *A Birder's Guide to the Rio Grande Valley of Texas* (L & P Photography, 1971).

# Utah

## Gunsight Peak (near Clarkston)

**Spring Flights:** Information unavailable.
**Autumn Flights:** Fair.

**Description:** An 8,244-foot-high (2,473 meter) peak at the southwestern corner of the Clarkston mountain range. Visibility is restricted, but some migrating raptors can be seen.

**Access:** From Logan drive north on Highway 91 to Smithfield. Turn left at the traffic light and drive about 15 miles (24 kilometers) to the town of Clarkston. At the northwest corner of the town take an unpaved road north out of town. Drive for several miles (kilometers), then turn left at the fork, heading westward toward the Clarkston range. Park at the end of the road and hike up Winter Canyon to the top of the ridge. The peak (Gunsight Peak) is located at the extreme western end of the range. The 4 miles (6.4 kilometers) of hiking required to reach the site is rigorous and takes about 2.5 hours.

**Reference:** None.

## Hyde Park Knoll (near Hyde Park)

**Spring Flights:** Fair.

**Autumn Flights:** Fair.

**Description:** An exposed area at an elevation of 7,100 feet (2,130 meters) on the western slope of the Bear River range. The site is most productive for accipiters and American Kestrels in September.

**Access:** From Logan drive north on 800 East Street for about 2 miles (3.2 kilometers) to the town of Hyde Park. At the first intersection turn right (east) and continue on the paved road, which becomes unpaved after about 0.5 mile (0.8 kilometer). Remain on the main unpaved road until you arrive at the mouth of a canyon (about 2 miles or 3.2 kilometers). Park there and walk to the top of the knoll north of the canyon. It is about 0.75 mile (1.2 kilometers) and some 1,500 vertical feet (450 meters) to the top. Most hawks pass high overhead and to the east further up the mountain face.

**Reference:** None.

## Promontory Point (near Brigham City)

**Spring Flights:** Information unavailable.

**Autumn Flights:** Fair (only for small accipiters).

**Description:** A mountain peak in the Southern Promontory Mountains at an elevation of 6,400 feet (1,920 meters). Observers enjoy watching hawks (mostly accipiters) heading toward Great Salt Lake.

**Access:** At the north end of Brigham City drive west on Route 83. Follow the signs to Golden Spike National Historic Site. After turning off Route 83 take a left at the next fork (after about 1.5 miles or 2.4 kilometers) and drive south for about 25 miles (40 kilometers) to the tip of the Promontory peninsula (Promontory

Point). This spot is shown on many road maps. Hike north for about 3 miles (4.8 kilometers) to the highest peak at the southwestern end of the peninsula. Hawks may be seen in all directions from this spot. However, the site is private property and permission may be needed to enter the property.
**Reference:** None.

## Utah Valley Hawk Migration Lookouts (near Orem)

**Spring Flights:** Information unavailable.
**Autumn Flights:** Fair.
**Description:** A scenic overlook or parking area, and a knoll, with views over a nearby valley and mountain range.
**Access:** From Interstate 15 at Orem take the most northern Orem exit marked State Highway 52 to U.S. 189 and drive east on State Highway 52 (8th North) for 3.6 miles (5.7 kilometers) to the junction with U.S. Route 189. Turn left onto U.S. Route 189 and drive northeast for 2 miles (3.2 kilometers) to the Squaw Peak Trail. Follow the trail for 4.1 miles (6.5 kilometers) to where the road forms a T intersection. Take a right-hand turn at the T and continue a short distance to a scenic overlook or parking area from which migrating hawks can be seen. Alternatively turn left at the T intersection and drive for 1.9 miles (3 kilometers)—the paved road ends just past the Hope Picnic Area—to a turnout and gravel parking area on the right side of the road. Park here and hike along the contours at the northeast to a knoll overlooking the valley from which hawk watching is also done. Birds approach from the north-northeast above and below the vantage points. West winds produce the largest flights which seem to appear in peak numbers during the second and third weeks of September.
**Reference:** None.

## Wellsville Mountain Hawk Lookout

**Spring Flights:** Poor.
**Autumn Flights:** Good.
**Description:** A knoll (elevation over 8,500 feet or 2,550 meters) on top of the northern end of the Wellsville Mountain range from which observers enjoy splendid panoramic views. Hawks usually fly along the west side of the range at eye level or slightly below. Most migrants are seen between September and late October.
**Access:** At the junction of Routes 89 and 30 in Logan, drive west on 2nd North Street (Route 30) for 6 blocks to 6th West Street. Turn left (south) and continue for 8 blocks to 6th South Street. Turn right (west) and drive about 8 miles (12.8 kilometers) to the hamlet of Mendon. The road turns south at the end of town. Continue 2 blocks to 3rd North Street and turn right. Then drive

through town (4 blocks) and continue to the point where the road is no longer paved. Stay to the right (west) and drive 3 miles (4.8 kilometers) on this unpaved road until you arrive at the edge of a maple forest. Park here and look for a sign pointing to Deep Canyon Trail to the left. Hike 3.5 miles (5.6 kilometers) up Deep Canyon to the top of the ridge. Turn right (north) and hike another 0.7 mile (1.1 kilometers) along the ridge to the highest point. The hike to the lookout requires about 2.5 hours; the return to the parking area requires about 1.5 hours.

**References:** *Southwest Hawk Watch Newsletter,* 1978, 2 (1):2–3; *American Birds,* 1978, 32 (2):236–37.

# Vermont

## Camel's Hump (near Waterbury)

**Spring Flights:** Information unavailable.
**Autumn Flights:** Good.
**Description:** An exposed ledge with views over a broad valley.
**Access:** From Waterbury drive west on U.S. Route 2 to Jonesville, cross the Winooski River, then follow the first left onto a minor road for 2.5 miles (4 kilometers) to the Bamforth Ridge Trail sign on the right. Walk along this trail for about 2 miles (3.2 kilometers) to a point where it tops out on the first spruce ridge. The exposed ledge is located nearby.
**Reference:** *GBF.*

## Glebe Mountain (near Londonderry)

**Spring Flights:** Poor.
**Autumn Flights:** Fair.
**Description:** A boulder-strewn slope at the top of Glebe Mountain from which observers enjoy good views from the southwest through the northeast.
**Access:** From Londonderry drive east on Route 11 for about 2 miles (3.2 kilometers) and follow signs to the Magic Mountain Ski Area base lodge. Park there. Then begin a long, and sometimes strenuous, hike up the trail under the ski lift in front of (and to the right of) the lodge. When you reach mid-station follow the trail leading to the right, then the maintenance road which gradually climbs the ridge. Hawk watching is done from the top of the steep boulder-strewn slope overlooking the road.
**Reference:** None.

## Hogback Mountain (between Bennington and Brattleboro)

**Spring Flights:** Information unavailable.

**Autumn Flights:** Fair.

**Description:** An overview beside the road with excellent views toward the south.

**Access:** From Bennington drive east on Route 9. The highway crosses Hogback Mountain and the overview beside the road is obvious.

**References:** *AHF; GEHW.*


## Putney Mountain (near Putney)

**Spring Flights:** Poor.

**Autumn Flights:** Fair.

**Description:** An open mountaintop (and highest point) on Putney Mountain from which observers enjoy good views in all directions.

**Access:** The following directions may not be completely accurate but they are the only ones available. Local residents may be able to provide additional information. From the intersection of West Hill Road and Westminster Road (both of which lack name signs) 1 mile (1.6 kilometers) northwest of the center of the village of Putney, drive northwest to unpaved Brookline Road (perhaps also unmarked) which apparently leads to the top of the mountain at which point there is a turnoff for a parking area. Park there, then walk northward along a trail for about 1 mile (1.6 kilometers) to the exposed lookout from which hawk watching is done. During the autumn hawk-watching season (or perhaps only for several weekends) local hawk watchers apparently place directional signs at key intersections to guide visitors to the lookout.

**Reference:** *Newsletter Southeastern Vermont Audubon Society,* 1977, (October):1.


## Snake Mountain (near Addison)

**Spring Flights:** Poor.

**Autumn Flights:** Fair (perhaps occasionally good).

**Description:** The exposed top of a rocky cliff on the west side of the mountain providing views of the Champlain Valley and Lake Champlain.

**Access:** From the junction of Routes 22A and 17 at Addison, drive south on Route 22A to Willmarth Road. Turn east onto Willmarth Road and continue to the end of the road. Park in a suitable spot. Then walk through a gate protecting a road that leads up the mountain to a T in the road. Turn left at the T and continue walking left for the remaining distance to the top of the mountain from which observations are made. The hike up the mountain requires 45 minutes or more.

**Reference:** None.

# Virginia

## Big Schloss (near Luray)

**Spring Flights:** Information unavailable.
**Autumn Flights:** Good.
**Description:** A prominent rocky outcropping from which observers have 330 degrees of unrestricted visibility.
**Access:** From Luray, Virginia, follow Route 675 northwest about 25 miles (40 kilometers) to the Wolf Gap Recreation Park. Alternatively from Wardensville, West Virginia, drive west on Route 55 to the junction with Route 259. Turn south on Route 259 for some 13 or 14 miles (about 21 kilometers) into Wolf Gap. Park in a suitable location, then walk up the Blue Trail for about 2 miles (3.2 kilometers) to the lookout on top of Big Schloss.
**Reference:** None.

## Chincoteague National Wildlife Refuge (near Chincoteague)

**Spring Flights:** Information unavailable.
**Autumn Flights:** Fair.
**Description:** A barrier beach island along which migrating falcons and other raptors appear. Observations are made from the vicinity of two observation blinds on opposite sides of a freshwater pond along Wildlife Drive, or from the barrier beach where Peregrine Falcons sometimes appear.
**Access:** From Pocomoke City, Maryland, drive south on U.S. Route 13 to Oak Hill, Virginia. Turn east onto Route 175 and drive to the town of Chincoteague. When entering the town on Route 175 turn left onto Main Street and continue for 7 blocks. Then turn right onto Maddox Boulevard and follow it to the refuge headquarters or information center located 0.5 mile (0.8 kilometer) beyond the Assateague Channel bridge. The refuge's Wildlife Drive is open from 6:00 A.M. to 3:00 P.M. for hiking and biking, and from 3:00 P.M. to sunset for auto traffic.
**Reference:** *NHMA,* 1978, 3 (2):10–12.

## Harvey's Knob Overlook (near Buchanan)

**Spring Flights:** Information unavailable.
**Autumn Flights:** Excellent.
**Description:** An overlook along the Blue Ridge Parkway with views of surrounding valleys. Diagonally across the parkway is Pine Tree Overlook, which sometimes is used in combination with hawk watching from Harvey's Knob Overlook.
**Access:** From the junction of Interstate 81 and Route 43 at Buchanan, drive south on Route 43 to the Blue Ridge Parkway, then west on the parkway to milepost 95.3 (kilometer 152.4) and

the Harvey's Knob Overlook.
**Reference:** *NHMA*, 1976, 1 (2):14–15.

## Humpback Rocks (near Charlottesville)

**Spring Flights:** None.
**Autumn Flights:** Good.
**Description:** A summit of the Blue Ridge overlooking the Valley of Virginia.
**Access:** From Charlottesville drive west on Interstate 64 or U.S. Route 250 to the top of the Blue Ridge. Then continue south for 6 miles (9.6 kilometers) on the Blue Ridge Parkway to the parking area below Humpback Rocks on the left side of the road. Park there and hike for about 0.75 mile (1.2 kilometers) up a steep trail to the Humpback Rocks summit from which hawk watching is done.
**Reference:** *GBF*.

## Irish Creek Overlook (near Buena Vista)

**Spring Flights:** Information unavailable.
**Autumn Flights:** Poor.
**Description:** An overlook along the Blue Ridge Parkway with views of the surrounding valleys.
**Access:** From Buena Vista drive east on U.S. Route 60 to the Blue Ridge Parkway, then east on the parkway to milepost 42.4 (kilometer 67.8) and the Irish Creek Overlook.
**Reference:** *NHMA*, 1976, 1 (2):15.

## Kennedy Peak (near Luray)

**Spring Flights:** Information unavailable.
**Autumn Flights:** Excellent.
**Description:** A low tower-shelter on the peak of Mount Kennedy with good visibility from the north through the southwest but with restricted visibility to the west and northwest.
**Access:** From Luray drive west on Route 211. After passing a Holiday Inn continue for about 1.5 miles (2.4 kilometers) to the off-ramp leading to Route 340S. Take that exit. Turn left at the bottom of the ramp, continue for 0.3 mile (0.4 kilometer) on Route 340, then turn right onto Route 675. Follow Route 675 for about 7 miles (11.2 kilometers), crossing the south fork of the Shenandoah River. At the end of the bridge turn left, continue for 0.3 mile (0.4 kilometer), then turn right. Drive about 2.5 miles (4 kilometers) to the Kennedy Peak parking area. Park, then walk on the trail leading off the right side of the road following the signs marked for Kennedy Peak (2 miles or 3.2 kilometers). Walk 1.8 miles (2.8 kilometers), then turn right where the trail begins a long descent

slightly to the left, at a wooden marker. Continue up a steep incline to the peak some 300 yards (270 meters) away.
**Reference:** *NHMA, 1976, 1 (2):14–15.*

## Kiptopeke

**Spring Flights:** None.
**Autumn Flights:** Good.
**Description:** The tip of the Delmarva Peninsula about a mile (1.6 kilometers) south of the town of Kiptopeke.
**Access:** From Norfolk to the south, or more northern points on the Delmarva Peninsula, follow Route 13 to the southern end of the peninsula and look for local directional signs pointing to Kiptopeke.
**Reference:** *AHF; GEHW.*

## Mendota Fire Tower (near Hansonville)

**Spring Flights:** None.
**Autumn Flights:** Excellent.
**Description:** A fire tower providing exposed views from the summit of Clinch Mountain.

*Mendota Fire Tower, Va.*

**Access:** From Abingdon drive north on Route 19 (Alternate 58) to Hansonville, then follow Route 802 to Route 614 and continue to the top of the mountain. Park in the saddle at the top, and hike on the trail on the right for about 15 minutes until the fire tower is reached.

**References:** *AHF; GEHW.*

## Mills Gap Overlook (near Buchanan)

**Spring Flights:** Information unavailable.
**Autumn Flights:** Excellent.
**Description:** An overlook along the Blue Ridge Parkway with views of surrounding valleys.
**Access:** From the junction of Interstate 81 and Route 43 at Buchanan, drive south on Route 43 to the Blue Ridge Parkway, then west on the parkway to milepost 91.8 (kilometer 146.8) and the Mills Gap Overlook. Observe from there.
**Reference:** *NHMA,* 1977, 2 (2):17.

## Monterey Mountain (near Monterey)

**Spring Flights:** Information unavailable.
**Autumn Flights:** Good.
**Description:** An open ridge in a pasture on top of Monterey Mountain providing good overhead views as well as toward the north and east.
**Access:** From the junction of U.S. Routes 220 and 250 at Monterey, drive west on U.S. Route 250 for 3 miles (4.8 kilometers) to the top of the mountain. Park in a space beside a picnic table at the mountaintop. Then cross a fence at the table and walk north for 75 yards (67.5 meters) to an open ridge in the pasture from which hawk watching is done.
**Reference:** *Raven,* 1971, 42 (4):62.

## Purgatory Mountain Overlook (near Buchanan)

**Spring Flights:** Information unavailable.
**Autumn Flights:** Excellent.
**Description:** A roadside overlook along the Blue Ridge Parkway with excellent views of valleys and ridges (including Purgatory Mountain) toward the north.
**Access:** From the junction of Interstate 81 and Route 43 at Buchanan, drive south on Route 43 to the Blue Ridge Parkway, then west on the parkway for a few miles (kilometers) to the well-marked Purgatory Mountain Overlook just beyond milepost 92 (kilometer 147.8). Observe from there toward Purgatory Mountain in the distance.
**References:** *Virginia Society of Ornithology Newsletter,* 1972, 18 (5):2–3; *AHF.*

*Purgatory Mountain Overlook, Va.*

## Rockfish Gap (near Waynesboro)

**Spring Flights:** Information unavailable.
**Autumn Flights:** Fair.
**Description:** This lookout, sometimes called Afton Mountain, is the parking lot of a Holiday Inn at the intersection of milepost (kilometer) zero on the Blue Ridge Parkway, U.S. Route 250, and Interstate 64.
**Access:** From Waynesboro drive south on U.S. Route 250 to the Blue Ridge Parkway and the Holiday Inn parking lot at the junction of the previously mentioned highways. Observe from the parking lot.
**References:** *Redstart,* 1953, 20 (3):39–54; *AHF; NHMA,* 1976, 1 (2):14–15.

## Sunset Fields Overlook (near Bedford)

**Spring Flights:** Information unavailable.
**Autumn Flights:** Fair.
**Description:** An overlook along the Blue Ridge Parkway with overhead views. Trees block visibility into the surrounding valleys.
**Access:** From Bedford drive north on Route 43 to the junction with the Blue Ridge Parkway, then west on the parkway to milepost 87.4 (kilometer 139.8) and the Sunset Fields Overlook.
**Reference:** *NHMA,* 1977, 2 (2):17.

## Thunder Ridge Overlook (near Big Island)

**Spring Flights:** Information unavailable.
**Autumn Flights:** Excellent.
**Description:** An overlook along the Blue Ridge Parkway with views of surrounding valleys. Trees partly block visibility.
**Access:** From Big Island drive north on U.S. Route 501 for a few miles (kilometers) to the junction with the Blue Ridge Parkway, then drive west on the parkway to milepost 74.7 (kilometer 119.5) and the Thunder Ridge Overlook. Observe from there.
**Reference:** *NHMA,* 1976, 1 (2):14–15.

## Turkey Mountain (near Amherst)

**Spring Flights:** Information unavailable.
**Autumn Flights:** Excellent.
**Description:** The side of a dead-end road overlooking pastures and farmland on Turkey Mountain. Hawks approach from the north and pass over the lookout or to one side of it.
**Access:** From Lynchburg drive north on U.S. Route 29 for about 15 miles (24 kilometers) to the junction with State Route 151. Turn left onto Route 151 and continue for about 2 miles (3.2 kilometers) to Route 610. Turn left onto Route 610 and continue for about 1 mile (1.6 kilometers) to the second unpaved road on the right (Route 738). Turn right and follow Route 738 for a few hundred feet (meters) until you reach the spot with a view of Turkey Mountain to the right. Park and view from the side of the road.
**Reference:** *NHMA,* 1976, 2 (2):16–17.

## Virginia Coast Reserve

**Spring Flights:** Information unavailable.
**Autumn Flights:** Good.
**Description:** A chain of 9 undisturbed barrier beach islands, and 4 interior islands, extending along the Delmarva Peninsula from the Virginia-Maryland border southward to the mouth of Chesapeake Bay. Parramore, Revel's, and Ship Shoal islands are closed to public use except by special permission. Day use is permitted, however, on Metomkin, Cedar, Sandy, Hog, Rogue, Cogg, Godwin, Myrtle, Mink, and Smith islands. The best raptor-viewing area on each island is generally at the southern tip of the beach. Accipiters and falcons are the most common autumn migrants. About 10 species of hawks also winter on the islands.
**Access:** The islands of the reserve can be reached only by boat. Since the channels around the islands are frequently dangerous, people wishing to visit the reserve are encouraged to contact the reserve manager (c/o The Nature Conservancy, Brownsville, Nassawadox, Va. 23413) for full details concerning the best

navigation routes to follow to the islands, information on possible guide services, and limitations concerning island use.
**Reference:** *Virginia Coast Reserve Study* (The Nature Conservancy, 1976).

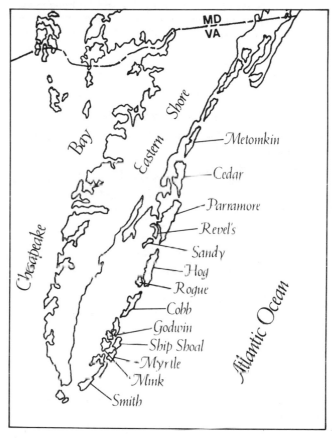

The islands of the Virginia Coast Reserve.
Map courtesy of the Nature Conservancy.

# West Virginia

## Backbone Mountain (near Thomas)

**Spring Flights:** Information unavailable.
**Autumn Flights:** Fair.
**Description:** A scenic roadside overlook on Backbone Mountain.
**Access:** From Thomas drive north on U.S. Route 219 for 4.2 miles (6.7 kilometers) to the overlook beside the road. Observe from there.
**References:** *Redstart,* 1953, 20 (3):39–54; *AHF.*

# Bear Rocks (in Monongahela National Forest)

**Spring Flights:** Information unavailable.
**Autumn Flights:** Good.
**Description:** A rocky outcropping on the Allegheny Front overlooking the Dolly Sods Scenic Area. Easterly and southerly winds are most productive.

*Bear Rocks, W. Va.*

**Access:** From the Dolly Sods Picnic Area in Monongahela National Forest drive north on Forest Service Road 75 past the Red Creek Camp Ground to the parking area for Bear Rocks. Park there and walk on the path for a short distance to the lookout rocks from which hawk watching is done.
**References:** *AHF; GEHW; Redstart,* 1974, 41 (4):119–20.

# Centennial Park (near Thomas)

**Spring Flights:** Information unavailable.
**Autumn Flights:** Fair.
**Description:** A roadside overlook and park (elevation about 3,000 feet or 900 meters) on Backbone Mountain providing observers with broad views of a valley toward the north and northeast.
**Access:** From Thomas drive west on U.S. Route 219 for 4.7 miles (7.5 kilometers) to Centennial Park located beside the highway. Hawk watching is done from the park's overlook.
**References:** *Redstart,* 1953, 20 (3):39–54; 1976, 43 (3):116.

## Cheat Mountain (near Mace)

**Spring Flights:** Information unavailable.
**Autumn Flights:** Fair.
**Description:** Two roadside areas overlooking adjacent valleys. One area is located north of Mace, the other south of Mace.
**Access:** From Mace drive north or south on U.S. Route 219 for about a mile (1.6 kilometers) in either direction to the respective roadside recreation sites. Observe from either site.
**References:** *Redstart,* 1953, 20 (3):39–54; *AHF.*

## Hanging Rocks Fire Tower (near Waiteville)

**Spring Flights:** None.
**Autumn Flights:** Excellent.
**Description:** A fire tower built on a rocky outcropping on the crest of Peters Mountain.

*Hanging Rocks Fire Tower, W. Va.*

**Access:** By road about 3 miles (4.8 kilometers) northwest of Waiteville. From Route 311 in Paint Bush, Virginia, drive west on County Route 600 for 11 miles (17.6 kilometers) to Waiteville, West Virginia. Then turn right onto an unpaved road and continue 3.6 miles (5.7 kilometers) up Peters Mountain to an unpaved road on the left. Turn onto that road and park in a suitable spot. Then hike up a trail leading to the top of the mountain. Turn left at a T in the trail near some buildings and shortly thereafter climb a steep bank to a field. Follow the trail over the left side of the field and enter the forest on the left side via a narrow trail (sometimes overgrown at the entrance and for the first few hundred feet or meters). Walk along this trail for about 0.5 mile (0.8 kilometer) until the fire tower is reached. **References:** *Redstart,* 1970, 37 (3):82–86; 1975, 42 (4):114–17; *AHF; GEHW.*

## Middle Ridge (near Charleston)

**Spring Flights:** None.
**Autumn Flights:** Good.
**Description:** A 20-acre mowed hilltop (elevation 1,200 feet or 360 meters) surrounded on all sides by woodland. Observers have unrestricted views in all directions.
**Access:** From Interstate 79 at Charleston take the Oakwood Road exit and follow State Route 214 south for 3 miles (4.8 kilometers) to Kanawha Forest Road. Follow Kanawha Forest Road for 0.5 mile (0.8 kilometer) to Middle Fork. Take Middle Fork and follow it for 1 mile (1.6 kilometers) to Middle Ridge Road. Follow Middle Ridge Road (unpaved) for 3 miles (4.8 kilometers) uphill to the gate at Middle Ridge Farm. Enter and secure permission from the owners (Mr. and Mrs. Harvey Shreve, Jr.) to watch hawks from the previously mentioned mowed hilltop. Middle Ridge lookout, located on private property, is open to hawk watchers during the hours of 9:00 A.M. and 3:00 P.M. between 14 and 28 September. The best hawk flights have been seen between 20 and 22 September.
**Reference:** *Redstart,* 1970, 37 (4):115–16.

## North Mountain (near Gerrardstown)

**Spring Flights:** Information unavailable.
**Autumn Flights:** Fair.
**Description:** A fire tower on top of North Mountain providing good views of the surrounding area. Since this tower is not in service the lower section of the tower's ladder has been removed to prevent children from climbing the tower. However, hawk watchers can bring their own equipment to bridge the missing section of ladder and use the tower at their own risk.
**Access:** From Gerrardstown drive northwest on State Route 51 to its junction with State Route 45 at Mill Gap. Turn right onto State Route 45 and drive 2.9 miles (4.6 kilometers) to Secondary Route 45/8. Turn left onto Secondary Route 45/8 and continue for 0.3 mile (0.4 kilometer). Then turn left onto Secondary Route 45/14 and drive for 0.7 mile (1.1 kilometers) and park in a

suitable spot. Hike west for about a mile (1.6 kilometers) to the North Mountain fire tower. Alternatively contact the forest ranger (615 West King Street, Martinsburg, W.V.) for information on a forest road which leads to the tower.

**References:** *Redstart,* 1953, 20 (3):39–54; *AHF.*

## Paddy Knob (near Frost)

**Spring Flights:** Information unavailable.
**Autumn Flights:** Fair.
**Description:** A fire tower from which observers can view the surrounding area.
**Access:** From Frost drive east on West Virginia Route 84 for 4.6 miles (7.3 kilometers) to Frost Route 55. Follow that road for 2.3 miles (3.6 kilometers) to Paddy Knob. Since this tower is not in service, the lower section of the tower's ladder has been removed to prevent children from climbing the tower. However, hawk watchers can bring their own equipment to bridge the missing section of ladder and use the tower at their own risk.
**Reference:** *Redstart,* 1970, 37 (3):82–86.

# Wisconsin

## Cedar Grove Ornithological Station (near Cedar Grove)

**Spring Flights:** Fair.
**Autumn Flights:** Good.
**Description:** A high bluff near Lake Michigan or any spot near the lake shoreline with an unrestricted view.
**Access:** Drive east on U.S. Route 141 to the junction of Route 42 near Cedar Grove. Continue east on Route 141 for 0.5 mile (0.8 kilometer) to the point where the highway turns north. Turn onto a gravel road and continue eastward 0.25 mile (0.4 kilometer) toward Lake Michigan, then turn sharply north onto the first road on the left. Continue for 0.5 mile (0.8 kilometer). Cross Bahr Creek and park near the sanctuary. Presumably hawk watchers are not welcome in the sanctuary, but it may be possible to watch migrating hawks from the vicinity of the sanctuary itself.
**Reference:** *Wilson Bulletin,* 1961:171–92.

## Eagle Valley Nature Preserve (near Cassville)

**Spring Flights:** Good.
**Autumn Flights:** Good.
**Description:** A 5-acre prairie on top of a 300-foot-high (90 meter) bluff overlooking the Mississippi River. The lookout is part of

the 1,400-acre preserve. Large numbers of migrating Bald Eagles are seen in late November and early December, and again in February and early March.

**Access:** From Cassville follow County Route V V north for about 7 miles (11.2 kilometers) passing the Nelson Dewey State Park. Continue driving for another 0.5 mile (0.8 kilometer) past the Charlotte cemetery to unpaved Duncan Road, then turn left and follow Duncan Road for about a mile (1.6 kilometers) to the Nature Preserve entrance on the left in the valley. For additional details contact Eagle Valley Environmentalists, Inc., P.O. Box 155, Apple River, Ill. 61001.

**References:** *Eagle Valley News*, 1976, 5 (3):27–28; 1976, 5 (4):6.

## Harrington Beach State Park (near Port Washington)

**Spring Flights:** Information unavailable.
**Autumn Flights:** Good.
**Description:** An exposed vantage point along Lake Michigan at the northern end of the park.
**Access:** From Port Washington drive north on U.S. Route 141 for 5.5 miles (8.8 kilometers) to the village of Lake Church. Here turn east onto County Route D and continue to the parking area. Then walk to the lake shore from which hawk watching is done.
**Reference:** *GBF.*

## Schlitz Audubon Center (Milwaukee)

**Spring Flights:** Information unavailable.
**Autumn Flights:** Fair.
**Description:** Open fields near the shoreline of 'Lake Michigan.
**Access:** In Milwaukee drive north on U.S. Route 141 to State Route 100 (Brown Deer Road). Exit and drive east to the corner of North Lake Drive. The entrance to the center is on the right side of Brown Deer Road just east of North Lake Drive. Enter and continue to the headquarters. Park and ask about the best location for watching hawks in the sanctuary. The center is open Tuesdays through Saturdays.
**Reference:** *GBF.*

# Wyoming

## Indian Medicine Wheel (near Lovell)

**Spring Flights:** Information unavailable.
**Autumn Flights:** Good.

**Description:** A rounded knob on the eastern edge of the Big Horn National Forest providing observers with views over the Big Horn Basin and the northern portion of the Big Horn Mountains. Late August to mid-September is the best period to see migrating hawks. Clear weather is necessary.

**Access:** From Lovell drive east on alternate U.S. Route 14 for about 30 miles (48 kilometers) to the Indian Medicine Wheel (marked as a "point of interest" on state highway maps). Observers can drive within approximately 600 feet (180 meters) of the summit of the knob, then make an easy hike to the top.

**Reference:** None.

# Canada

## New Brunswick

### St. Andrews (near Calais, Maine)

**Spring Flights:** Fair.
**Autumn Flights:** Information unavailable.
**Description:** Exposed areas along the tidal inlet at the federal fisheries and ocean research station at the western end of town. Migrating Bald Eagles appear here, and a population of nesting Ospreys is also present.
**Access:** From Calais, Maine, on the United States-Canada border, drive east into New Brunswick on Highway 1 and continue for a few miles to the junction with Highway 127. Turn right (south) onto Highway 127 and follow it to St. Andrews where directions can be secured for reaching the research station and tidal inlet.
**Reference:** None.

## Nova Scotia

### Brier Island (near Digby)

**Spring Flights:** None.
**Autumn Flights:** Good.
**Description:** Open areas around either of two lighthouses. The North Point Light, in whose vicinity most observations are made, is on a rocky point 50 feet (15 meters) above sea level. An open area covered with heath-type vegetation surrounds the light. The vicinity of the South Light is sometimes more productive when weather changes force hawks to stop over on the island.
**Access:** From Digby drive on Route 217 for about 30 miles (48 kilometers) to East Ferry. Board a car ferry here (operating hourly) and cross to Long Island and the village of Tiverton. Continue on Route 217 for about 11 miles (17.6 kilometers) to Freeport. Here board another car ferry and cross to Westport—the only village on Brier Island. From Westport continue to the appropriate lighthouse. A good road runs from one end of the island to the other.
**References:** *The Birds of Nova Scotia* (Nova Scotia Museum, 1962); *AHF; GEHW.*

# Ontario

## Amherstburg

**Spring Flights:** Information unavailable.
**Autumn Flights:** Excellent.
**Description:** Two sites are suitable for watching migrating Broad-winged Hawks, and various other species, in the vicinity of Amherstburg. Many hawks can be seen from a point of land projecting into the Detroit River opposite the south end of Grosse Ile. Alternatively use the grounds of the Malden School along Route 18 east of Amherstburg.
**Access:** To reach the projection of land extending into the Detroit River drive west from the center of Amherstburg. To reach the Malden School drive east from Amherstburg on Route 18 to the school grounds. Observe from either location.
**References:** *Audubon Magazine*, 1962, 64 (1):44–45, 49; *AHF*.

## Cobourg

**Spring Flights:** Information unavailable.
**Autumn Flights:** Good.
**Description:** Full details are unavailable but exposed areas along the Lake Ontario shoreline probably are suitable observation points. Hawk flights are known to occur from Cobourg westward along Lake Ontario.
**Access:** From Toronto drive east on Route 401 to the exit for the town of Cobourg. Leave the main highway here and drive into town. Ask for directions to suitable exposed areas along the Lake Ontario shoreline where hawk watching can be done. Some exploration of the area will be necessary to locate productive spots which may change from day to day.
**References:** *Audubon Magazine*, 1962, 64 (1):44–45, 49; *AHF*.

## Grimsby

**Spring Flights:** Excellent.
**Autumn Flights:** Information unavailable.
**Description:** The tip of Beamer Point on the Niagara Escarpment overlooking the town of Grimsby.
**Access:** Grimsby is located at an exit along the Queen Elizabeth Way roughly halfway between Hamilton and St. Catharines. Leave the Queen Elizabeth Way at Casablanca Street and follow it south across railroad tracks to Road 81 (formerly Highway 8). Turn left (east) onto Road 81 and continue a short distance to Wolverton Street. Turn right (south) onto Wolverton Street and continue to Ridge Road West. Turn left (east) onto Ridge Road

West and continue to Quarry Road on the left. Turn into Quarry Road and follow it to the end at Beamer Point.
**Reference:** *NHMA,* 1978, 3 (1):10–13.

## Hawk Cliff (near Port Stanley)

**Spring Flights:** None.
**Autumn Flights:** Excellent.
**Description:** Fields near the edge of a 100-foot-high (30 meters) cliff at the edge of Lake Erie, or a wooded ravine inland about 0.25 mile (0.4 kilometer) from the lake.
**Access:** From St. Thomas drive south on Route 22 for about 8 miles (12.8 kilometers) directly to the cliffs overlooking Lake Erie.
**References:** *Search,* 1972, 2 (16):1–60; *AHF; GEHW.*

## Holiday Beach Provincial Park (near Windsor)

**Spring Flights:** None.
**Autumn Flights:** Excellent.
**Description:** A parking lot in the park next to the water.
**Access:** From Windsor, follow Highway 18 through Amherstburg. After crossing Big Creek continue for about 2 miles (3.2 kilometers) to the intersection of Route 18A. Turn right and continue for about 3 miles (4.8 kilometers) to the park entrance on the right. Enter and drive to the parking lot farthest from the park entrance. Observe from there.
**References:** *American Birds,* 1975, 29 (1):49–50; *GEHW.*

## Killarney Provincial Park (near Killarney)

**Spring Flights:** Information unavailable.
**Autumn Flights:** Good.
**Description:** Any exposed summit of ridge crests. Hawks generally follow a westward flight line, but Turkey Vultures appear to fly eastward.
**Access:** From Sudbury drive south on Highway 69 for about 20 miles (32 kilometers) to Highway 637. Turn west onto Highway 637 and continue for about 44 miles (70.4 kilometers) to the park entrance. Hiking trails and canoe routes run throughout the park and can be used to reach suitable hawk-watching sites such as those previously described.
**Reference:** None.

## Port Credit

**Spring Flights:** None.
**Autumn Flights:** Good.

**Description:** The vicinity of the Route 10 bridge over the Queen's Way.

**Access:** Drive about 15 miles (24 kilometers) southwest of Toronto on the Queen Elizabeth Way. At the junction of Provincial Route 10 turn onto it and continue to the bridge crossing the Queen's Way. Observe from this general area.

**References:** *Audubon Magazine,* 1962, 64 (1):44–45, 49; *AHW; GEHW.*

## Point Pelee National Park (near Leamington)

**Spring Flights:** None.

**Autumn Flights:** Excellent.

**Description:** The forest or open beach at the tip of the point, the vicinity of the park's Interpretive Center, or the open fields behind the maintenance compound.

**Access:** Drive south from Leamington for about 6 miles (9.6 kilometers) into the park.

**References:** *EBBA News,* 1961, 24 (2):25–26; *Wilson Bulletin,* 1966:122; *AHF; GEHW.*

## Rondeau Provincial Park (near Blenheim)

**Spring Flights:** None.

**Autumn Flights:** Excellent.

**Description:** Exposed areas on the park's south beach along Lake Erie. The site is particularly good for observing Sharp-shinned Hawks and Broad-winged Hawks.

**Access:** From Blenheim drive east on Highway 3 for a few miles (kilometers) to a road (probably marked) leading south into Rondeau Provincial Park. Upon entering the park drive about 6 miles (9.6 kilometers) to the southern end where a beach along Lake Erie is located. Hawk watching is done from there.

**Reference:** None.

## Tobermory (on the Bruce Peninsula in Lake Huron)

**Spring Flights:** Excellent.

**Autumn Flights:** Information unavailable.

**Description:** The vicinity of the ferry terminal (on the "Big Tub") in the village of Tobermory. The first two weeks in May are particularly good for hawk watching here.

**Access:** From Owen Sound drive west on Highway 21 for about 11 miles (17.6 kilometers) to the junction with Highway 6. Turn north onto Highway 6 and follow it about 61 miles (97.6 kilometers) to the village of Tobermory. Continue to the vicinity of the ferry terminal where hawk watching is done.

**Reference:** None.

# Quebec

## Ile Perrot (near Montreal)

**Spring Flights:** Fair.
**Autumn Flights:** Fair.
**Description:** An exposed area on the south side of Don Quichotte Road overlooking fields just east or west of a small wooded plateau. Occasionally hawk watching is also done at other points along Don Quichotte Road.
**Access:** From the western side of Montreal, follow Route 20 to Ile Perrot and continue to Don Quichotte Road. Turn east onto Don Quichotte Road and continue for about 2 or 3 miles (about 4 kilometers) toward Windmill Point (Pointe du Moulin). After crossing a small wooded plateau about 100 feet (30 meters) in elevation look for fields at the eastern side of the plateau. Observe from the south side of the road looking north across the road and fields.
**Reference:** *American Birds,* 1976, 30 (1):37.

## Morgan Arboretum (west of Montreal)

**Spring Flights:** Fair.
**Autumn Flights:** Good.
**Description:** A ridge at the top of Montreal Island along Highway 40 at the Ste. Anne de Bellevue exit. Observers on the ridge have good views north and south.
**Access:** Full details are unavailable, but one drives about 20 miles (32 kilometers) west from Montreal on Highway 40 to the Ste. Anne de Bellevue exit. Presumably one can then park at the arboretum and walk to the top of the ridge from which hawk watching is done. It may be possible to secure additional information at the arboretum.
**Reference:** *Birding News Survey,* 1978, 1 (1):13–14.

## Mount Royal (in Montreal)

**Spring Flights:** Fair.
**Autumn Flights:** Fair.
**Description:** An exposed area on the mountaintop near the cross.
**Access:** Full details are not available, but Mount Royal apparently is in the center of the city and easily located and visited.
**Reference:** *Birding News Survey,* 1978, 1 (1):13–14.

# Valleyfield

**Spring Flights:** Good.

**Autumn Flights:** Information unavailable.

**Description:** A small site at the western end of a bridge just west of Valleyfield at the eastern end of Lake St. Francis.

**Access:** From Valleyfield (about 60 miles or 96 kilometers southwest of Montreal) drive west on Highway 132 to the seaway lift bridge. Continue to the western end of the bridge where a small hawk-watching site is located at the junction of the seaway road. Observe from there.

**Reference:** *Birding News Survey,* 1978, 1 (1):13–14.

# Bald Eagle Viewing Areas United States

Bald Eagles are spectacular birds of prey worth watching during migration or at various gathering areas in winter. However, they are very sensitive to close human disturbance. Therefore, when visiting some of the sites discussed in the following pages, never approach Bald Eagles closer than about a quarter mile (0.4 kilometer). Under no circumstances should persons attempt to approach or disturb nesting eagles; nor should winter eagle roosts be approached closely or disturbed. There are severe federal penalties for doing so.

## Alaska

### Berners Bay (near Juneau)

**Raptors:** Bald Eagles feeding on Smelt runs.
**Viewing Season:** Early to mid-May.
**Description:** The shorelines of rivers running into Berners Bay in which Smelt provide abundant food for the eagles.
**Access:** From Juneau one can arrange a short charter flight to visit Berners Bay and the rivers entering the bay along which eagles feed.
**Reference:** *BEA.*

### Chilkat River (near Haines)

**Raptors:** Large concentrations of feeding Bald Eagles (maximum 3,000 per day).
**Viewing Season:** October through December.
**Description:** A shallow river, river shoreline, and the edges of dense surrounding forests.
**Access:** From Haines drive north on State Route 7 (Haines Highway) to mile marker 19 (kilometer 30.4) where large numbers of Bald Eagles can be seen along the river from the vicinity of a rockslide along the road.
**Reference:** *BEA.*

### Cook Inlet (near Anchorage)

**Raptors:** Bald Eagles.
**Viewing Season:** Year round with largest numbers appearing in mid-April.
**Description:** The shorelines and edges of forests bordering rivers that enter Cook Inlet.
**Access:** By private airplane flights to various small towns and

villages along Cook Inlet or by boat.
**Reference:** *BEA.*


## Glacier Bay National Monument

**Raptors:** Bald Eagles (over 100 active nests around Glacier Bay, and others elsewhere within the national monument boundaries).
**Viewing Season:** All year.
**Description:** An outstanding Bald Eagle viewing area set against a kaleidoscope of glaciers, sea, forests, muskegs, and high mountains. Eagle watching can be done from cruise ships, tour boats, or from the visitor facilities at the headquarters in Bartlett Cove.
**Access:** Glacier Bay is located 100 miles (160 kilometers) northwest of Juneau; it is reached by commercial airlines, private plane charters, summer cruise ships, and private boats.
**Reference:** None.


## Katmai National Monument

**Raptors:** Bald Eagles.
**Viewing Season:** Summer.
**Description:** The park's coast bordering the Shelikof Straits.
**Access:** The summer headquarters of Katmai National Monument are located at Brooks Camp about 406 miles (690 air kilometers) southwest of Anchorage. No visitor facilities are available. The area is accessible only by private or charter airplanes.
**Reference:** None.


## Klondike Gold Rush National Historical Park (near Skagway)

**Raptors:** Bald Eagles.
**Viewing Season:** Spring, summer, and autumn.
**Description:** Areas along the Taiya River in the park's Chilkoot Pass Unit as well as the vicinity of the towns of Skagway and Dyea bordering the Lynn Canal.
**Access:** Skagway is located in southwestern Alaska and is reached by commercial airlines, summer cruise ships, and the Alaska Marine Highway (Ferry) System. A road connecting Skagway with the Al-Can Highway is currently under construction but is not yet completed. Details on reaching the Taiya River area are available at the national park headquarters in Skagway.
**Reference:** None.


## Kodiak Island

**Raptors:** Bald Eagles.
**Viewing Season:** All year.

**Description:** The shorelines of various rivers and bays around the island.
**Access:** By ferry (from Homer or Anchorage) or airplane. There are no roads on the island. Additional information is available by writing to the Refuge Manager, Kodiak National Wildlife Refuge, Box 825, Kodiak, Alaska 99615.
**Reference:** *BEA.*

## Prince William Sound (near Anchorage)

**Raptors:** Bald Eagles.
**Viewing Season:** Year round with largest numbers appearing in mid-April.
**Description:** The shorelines and edges of forests bordering rivers that enter Prince William Sound.
**Access:** By private airplane flights to various small towns and villages along the sound, or by boat.
**Reference:** *BEA.*

## Seymour Eagle Management Area (on Admiralty Island)

**Raptors:** Nesting Bald Eagles (2 nests per mile).
**Viewing Season:** April through August.
**Description:** The shorelines of several small islands in Seymour Canal and on Admiralty Island in the Tongass National Forest. Also nearby shorelines of the Glass Peninsula bordering the Seymour Canal and other shoreline areas west of the canal.
**Access:** From Juneau or Sitka take a short charter flight to Admiralty Island.
**Reference:** *BEA.*

## Sitka National Historical Park

**Raptors:** Bald Eagles.
**Viewing Season:** All year.
**Description:** The harbor, park, and areas near the park including the old Russian settlement.
**Access:** Sitka is located on Baranof Island in southeastern Alaska and is reached by commercial airlines, summer cruise ships, and the Alaska Marine Highway (Ferry) System.
**Reference:** None.

## Stikine River (near Wrangell)

**Raptors:** Bald Eagles feeding on Smelt runs.
**Viewing Season:** Mid-April.

**Description:** The shorelines of the Stikine River in which Smelt runs provide abundant food for eagles.

**Access:** The Stikine River can be reached through Wrangell or Petersburg via the Marine Highway (Ferry) System.

**Reference:** *BEA.*

# Colorado

### Monte Vista National Wildlife Refuge (near Monte Vista)

**Raptors:** Bald Eagles (maximum 40 per day).

**Viewing Season:** Mid-December through February.

**Description:** Waterfowl ponds along the refuge's tour route; a marsh along the north side of County Road 7 Miles South; cottonwood trees along the southwestern corner of the refuge within sight of County Road 8 Miles South; and cottonwood trees along the east side of State Route 15 a short distance north of the refuge headquarters.

**Access:** From Monte Vista drive south on State Route 15 for about 5 miles (8 kilometers) to the refuge. Stop at the headquarters just off the highway and secure a visitor's map of the area and perhaps more details on the best spots for eagle viewing.

**Reference:** *WMBE.*

# Delaware

### Bombay Hook National Wildlife Refuge (near Smyrna)

Red-shouldered Hawk, Rough-legged Hawk, Northern Harrier, and American Kestrel.

**Viewing Season:** December through May.

**Description:** Trees and snags along the west side of Shearness Pool with viewing points available at safe distances along Whitehall Neck Road and the refuge tour route passing along the eastern side of Shearness Pond.

**Access:** From Smyrna drive south on U.S. Route 13 to the southern edge of town, then turn left at the well-marked sign pointing to Bombay Hook National Wildlife Refuge. Follow the signs for about 6 miles (9.6 kilometers) to the refuge. Stop at the refuge headquarters to secure current information and restrictions on eagle viewing. Never attempt to approach the eagle nests on foot.

**Reference:** *GBF.*

# Idaho

## Minidoka National Wildlife Refuge (near Rupert)

**Raptors:** Wintering Golden Eagles and Bald Eagles.
**Viewing Season:** November through March.
**Description:** Cottonwood trees adjacent to Lake Walcott at the refuge headquarters.
**Access:** From Rupert drive northeast on State Route 24 for 6 miles (9.6 kilometers), then turn east onto County Route 400-North (marked by a refuge sign) and continue another 6 miles (9.6 kilometers) to the refuge headquarters.
**Reference:** *WMBE.*

# Illinois

## Crab Orchard National Wildlife Refuge (near Marion)

**Raptors:** Concentrations of Bald Eagles.
**Viewing Season:** October through March with peak numbers appearing in late January and early February when Crab Orchard Lake is frozen.
**Description:** Trees near the shoreline of Crab Orchard Lake, open water near the refuge's water plant, and frozen sections of the lake where dead geese provide food for eagles.
**Access:** From the junction of Interstate 57 and U.S. Route 13 near Marion, drive west on Route 13 for about 5 miles (8 kilometers) to Wolf Creek Road. Turn left (south) onto Wolf Creek Road and continue for about 2 miles (3.2 kilometers) to the refuge water plant. Observe from a spot about ⅛ mile (0.2 kilometer) southeast of the water plant.
**Reference:** *WMBE.*

## Fort Edwards (Warsaw)

**Raptors:** Concentrations of Bald Eagles.
**Viewing Season:** November to mid-March.
**Description:** Open areas along Great River Road between Warsaw and Hamilton which provide views over the Mississippi River toward Missouri and upriver toward the islands and mouth of the Des Moines River. Sometimes dozens of eagles soar above the river on clear, mild winter days. Best viewing times are between late morning and early afternoon.
**Access:** From Hamilton ask directions to Great River Road and follow it southwestward to Warsaw and Fort Edwards.
**Reference:** None.

## Horseshoe Lake Conservation Area (near Olive Branch)

**Raptors:** Bald Eagles.
**Viewing Season:** Winter months.
**Description:** A 1,200-acre lake surrounded by fields and wooded areas.
**Access:** From Olive Branch, a small town in extreme southwestern Illinois, drive southeast on State Route 3 for about 2 miles (3.2 kilometers) to the sign marking the entrance road to the conservation area. Turn and follow the road to the lake shore from which observations are made.
**Reference:** *GBF.*


## Mississippi Lock and Dam 14 (near East Moline)

**Raptors:** Concentrations of Bald Eagles.
**Viewing Season:** Early winter.
**Description:** A public use area providing a view of the Mississippi River and a dam below which eagles gather.
**Access:** From the north side of East Moline drive north on Illinois Route 84 for 2.9 miles (4.6 kilometers) to the public use area. Park in the parking lot and look over the river for eagles.
**Reference:** *AB,* 1966, 140:32–34.


## Mississippi Lock and Dam 16 (near Illinois City)

**Raptors:** Concentrations of Bald Eagles.
**Viewing Season:** Winter.
**Description:** A gravel dike road running along the Mississippi River for almost 5 miles (8 kilometers) past the locks. Good views over the river are enjoyed, and eagles in the area can be easily seen.
**Access:** From the fire station in Illinois City follow Illinois Route 92 toward the Mississippi River for 7.8 miles (12.4 kilometers). Then turn right onto a gravel road near the approach to the bridge crossing the river. Follow this dike road (in good weather) for about 4.4 miles (7 kilometers) while keeping watch over the river for eagles.
**Reference:** *AB,* 1966, 140:32–34.


## Mississippi Lock and Dam 17 (near New Boston)

**Raptors:** Concentrations of Bald Eagles.
**Viewing Season:** Winter.
**Description:** An exposed area along the side of the Mississippi River upstream from New Boston, or the river front at New Boston.

**Access:** In New Boston drive to the river front from which eagles sometimes can be seen. Alternatively drive upstream on State Route 17 from the New Boston post office to the edge of town. At a roadside park turn right from State Route 17 onto County Road and drive 2.1 miles (3.3 kilometers) to the turnoff for the river. Turn onto the road leading to the river and continue another 1.5 miles (2.4 kilometers) to the river from which eagles frequently can be seen.
**Reference:** *AB,* 1966, 140:32–34.


## Montebello Conservation Area (near Hamilton)

**Raptors:** Concentrations of feeding Bald Eagles.
**Viewing Season:** November to mid-March, with peak numbers of birds frequently appearing in January during very cold weather.
**Description:** Open areas of water in the Mississippi River just below Lock and Dam 19 south of the Hamilton-Keokuk Bridge. The best viewing time is between one-half hour and two hours after sunrise.
**Access:** The Montebello Conservation Area is located west of Hamilton and just upriver from the bridge. From Hamilton drive west on U.S. Route 136 for a short distance. The park is situated to the right of the highway as one approaches the bridge.
**Reference:** *GBF.*


# Iowa

## Bellevue

**Raptors:** Bald Eagles.
**Viewing Season:** Winter.
**Description:** A public boat landing overlooking the Mississippi River.
**Access:** From Bellevue drive south on U.S. Route 52 for about a mile (1.6 kilometers) to the public boat landing. Park there and look for eagles downstream or across the river.
**Reference:** *WBMR.*


## Mississippi Lock and Dam 10 (Guttenburg)

**Raptors:** Bald Eagles.
**Viewing Season:** Winter.
**Description:** Open water between islands in the main river channel below the dam. Also trees beside the main river channel.
**Access:** In Guttenburg drive along U.S. Route 52 to a point in or near the town where the dam and river can be seen from the highway. Look for eagles from this spot. Alternatively drive or

hike to the top of the bluff at Guttenburg and look for eagles along the river or perched in trees beside it. An excellent view of the Eagle Valley Nature Preserve, located across the river, also can be enjoyed.

**Reference:** *WBMR.*

## Mississippi Lock and Dam 11 (Dubuque)

**Raptors:** Bald Eagles.
**Viewing Season:** Winter.
**Description:** Open areas on the river near the toll bridge, areas near an island south of the Route 20 bridge, or bluffs south of East Dubuque, Ill.
**Access:** In Dubuque drive to the toll bridge crossing the Mississippi River. Park in a suitable spot and look for eagles just south of the bridge; or follow U.S. Route 20 east to the bridge crossing the river and look for eagles sitting near an island south of the bridge; or drive south of East Dubuque, Ill., on U.S. Route 20 for 3 or 4 miles (about 5.5 kilometers) to some bluffs along the highway and look for eagles soaring overhead.
**Reference:** *WBMR.*

## Mississippi Lock and Dam 12 (Bellevue)

**Raptors:** Concentrations of Bald Eagles.
**Viewing Season:** Mid-February.
**Description:** Open areas along the Mississippi River below the locks and dam.
**Access:** Various spots along Iowa Routes 52 and 67 near Bellevue provide views of the locks and a few eagles. A public boat landing a mile (1.6 kilometers) south of Bellevue along Routes 56 and 67 is especially productive for eagle watching.
**Reference:** *AB,* 1966, 140:32–34.

## Mississippi Lock and Dam 15 (Davenport)

**Raptors:** Concentrations of Bald Eagles.
**Viewing Season:** Winter.
**Description:** Several sites are suitable for eagle viewing including a downtown parking levee overlooking the dam and river, and Cedar Island (a city park) in the river.
**Access:** From downtown Davenport drive to the parking levee or to Cedar Island and view from either location. Alternatively follow 18th Avenue in Rock Island, Illinois, to its west end and look over the river toward a small island beside Cedar Island, Iowa, where eagles often gather.
**Reference:** *AB,* 1966, 140:32–34.

## Victory Park (Keokuk)

**Raptors:** Concentrations of Bald Eagles.
**Viewing Season:** November to mid-March with peak numbers of birds frequently appearing in January during very cold weather.
**Description:** A park overlooking the Mississippi River where eagles gather in open water to feed.
**Access:** From the center of Keokuk drive east on Main Street for 8 blocks, then turn right into the park.
**Reference:** *GBF.*

# Kansas

## Quivira National Wildlife Refuge

**Raptors:** Concentrations of Bald Eagles.
**Viewing Season:** Early October to mid-March, with concentrations usually occurring from mid-December to mid-January.
**Description:** A 21,820-acre refuge with a variety of habitats including marshes, lakes, and rangeland. Eagle watching can be done with a telescope from the vicinity of the refuge office as the birds sit on the ice.
**Access:** By road 12 miles (19.2 kilometers) north of Stafford.
**Reference:** *WMBL.*

# Kentucky

## Lake Barkley State Resort Park and Land Between the Lakes Recreation Area (near Cadiz)

**Raptors:** Bald Eagles, Golden Eagles, Red-tailed Hawks, Red-shouldered Hawks, and Rough-legged Hawks.
**Viewing Season:** From mid-November to mid-March. The largest numbers of Bald Eagles are seen in January and February.
**Description:** Lake Barkley State Resort Park, just east of Land Between the Lakes Recreation Area, annually holds an "Eagle Weekend" in February during which organized eagle-viewing field trips and programs are provided for the public. Eagle viewing is done in the nearby 170,000-acre Land Between the Lakes Recreation Area where eagles tend to gather along the wooded shorelines of the bays and inlets along the various lakes. The Honker Bay and Fulton Bay areas along Lake Barkley are perhaps the best locations for observing wintering Bald Eagles, but other areas are also productive.
**Access:** From Cadiz drive west on Routes 68 and 80 to the Lake Barkley State Resort Park where naturalists can provide additional information on eagle viewing. Alternatively drive west on Routes 68 and 80 to the information station at the junction of

Routes 80 and 453 (called The Trace) where information, maps, and other materials are also available.

**References:** *WMBE; GBF.*

# Maryland

## Blackwater National Wildlife Refuge (near Cambridge)

**Raptors:** Bald Eagles (nesting); other eastern raptors.
**Viewing Season:** All year.
**Description:** Dead snags along the edge of the marsh behind the refuge visitors' center, or an observation tower along the road behind the public picnic area and rest-room facilities from which observers enjoy excellent views of the marshes on which eagles are seen frequently.
**Access:** From Cambridge drive south on State Route 16 for 7 miles (11.2 kilometers) to the village of Church Creek. Turn left there onto State Route 335 and continue for 4 miles (6.4 kilometers) to the refuge sign. Turn left at the sign and continue another 2 miles (3.2 kilometers) to the refuge visitors' center where full information and restrictions on eagle viewing can be secured. Never attempt to approach the eagle nests on foot. From September through May the visitors' center is open from 8:00 A.M. to 4:30 P.M. (Monday through Saturday) and from 10:00 A.M. to 4:30 P.M. on Sunday; it is closed Christmas Day.
**Reference:** *GBF.*

# Massachusetts

## Quabbin Reservoir (near Belchertown)

**Raptors:** Wintering Bald Eagles; occasionally Golden Eagles.
**Viewing Season:** January through March.
**Description:** A high point at the south end of the reservoir known as the Enfield Lookout from which observers look over two valleys of the reservoir. Eagles usually can be seen feeding on the ice if a telescope or binoculars are used. *Warning:* Never leave the lookout and attempt to approach the birds on the ice.
**Access:** From Exit 8 (Palmer exit) of the Massachusetts Turnpike drive north on Route 32 for about 8 miles (12.8 kilometers) to the junction of Routes 32 and 9 in the town of Ware. Turn left onto Route 9 and continue for about 3 miles (4.8 kilometers) toward Belchertown, to a well-marked Quabbin Reservoir sign. Turn onto the road and follow the signs for about 1.25 miles (2 kilometers) to the well-marked Enfield Lookout. Observe from there.
**Reference:** *WMBE.*

*Bald Eagles at Quabbin Reservoir, Mass.*

# Minnesota

## Mississippi Lock and Dam 2 (near Hastings)

**Raptors:** Bald Eagles.
**Viewing Season:** Winter months.
**Description:** The bridge over which Routes 10 and 61 cross the Mississippi River.
**Access:** From Hastings follow Routes 10 and 61 to the Mississippi River. Watch for eagles while crossing the bridge, or park at suitable sites near the bridge and explore the nearby riverbanks for eagles.
**Reference:** *WBMR.*

## Mississippi Lock and Dam 3 (near Red Wing)

**Raptors:** Bald Eagles.
**Viewing Season:** Early to mid-December.
**Description:** Islands in the Mississippi River south of Red Wing; Lake Pepin near the mouth of the Chippewa River; or trees close to bluffs beside Routes 61 and 63.
**Access:** From Red Wing drive south on Routes 61 and 63 to a point just south of town where the islands can be seen in the nearby river, or drive to trees beside the highway which sometimes serve as eagle roosts.
**Reference:** *WBMR.*

# Missouri

## Mississippi Lock and Dam 24 (Clarksville)

**Raptors:** Concentrations of Bald Eagles.
**Viewing Season:** Winter months.
**Description:** Exposed sections of the Mississippi River along the Clarksville business district or trees on nearby islands in mid-river.
**Access:** Park at any convenient location near the river in Clarksville and then walk to the riverbank from which eagles often can be seen flying low over the water or perched in trees on nearby islands.
**Reference:** *AB,* 1966, 140:32–34.


## Squaw Creek National Wildlife Refuge

**Raptors:** Large concentrations (maximum 263 per day) of wintering Bald Eagles.
**Viewing Season:** November through February. Peak numbers occur in January and February.
**Description:** Three areas on the refuge are frequented by eagles and can be studied from refuge roads and/or observation towers. An older stand of cottonwood forest near the southwestern end of the Northeast Pool is used as a night roost, and eagles can be seen flying in this area from the South Pool in early evening. During the day a smaller willow forest bordering the north edge of the South Pool is used as a loafing area by large numbers of eagles. Finally eagles also use the South Pool as a hunting area.
**Access:** Entrance to the refuge is reached a few miles (kilometers) south of Mound City off Route 159. Maps of the refuge are available at the headquarters building.
**Reference:** *WMBE.*


## Swan Lake National Wildlife Refuge (near Sumner)

**Raptors:** Bald Eagles (maximum 100 birds per day).

**Viewing Season:** Early October to late March, with peak numbers appearing in mid- to late December. Occasionally large numbers of eagles also appear in late February if a winter fish kill occurs.

**Description:** The levee road adjacent to the west side of Swan Lake connecting the refuge headquarters with State Route RA, or the high observation tower adjacent to the refuge headquarters from which observers enjoy fine views over Swan Lake. Eagles can be seen feeding on the frozen lake with the aid of binoculars or telescopes. The best time to view the birds is in the morning.
**Access:** From Sumner drive south on State Route RA for about 1 mile (1.6 kilometers) to the refuge sign and road leading to the

refute. Turn onto the entrance road and continue for about 1.5 miles (2.4 kilometers) to the headquarters, watching along the way for eagles on Swan Lake. A visit to the refuge headquarters will produce the most current information on the status of eagles on the refuge.

**Reference:** *WMBE.*

# Montana

## Glacier National Park

**Raptors:** Large concentrations (maximum 373 per day) of Bald Eagles feeding on Kokanee Salmon.

**Viewing Season:** Late September to mid-December. Mid-November is the best period for seeing the largest number of eagles.

*Bald Eagles at Glacier National Park, Mont.*

The birds begin arriving along Lower McDonald Creek just before dawn and feed as soon as there is enough light to see. Feeding continues actively for about two hours, after which many of the birds remain perched in trees along the creek until about 30 minutes before sunset when they migrate to several well established roost sites nearby.

**Description:** The National Park Service has established two public eagle observation areas, Apgar Bridge and Quarter Circle Bridge, overlooking Lower McDonald Creek (a narrow, winding 2.4-mile-long [3.8 kilometers] creek draining Lake McDonald) near the western boundary of Glacier National Park in northwestern Montana. People using these public observation areas must remain in designated places because the eagles are extremely sensitive to human disturbance. Nobody should attempt to approach the birds closer than 500 yards (450 meters).

**Access:** From West Glacier (on U.S. Route 2) drive north into the park and stop at the headquarters or information center for details about eagle watching. Then continue to the Apgar Bridge or Quarter Circle Bridge viewing areas.

**Reference:** "A Management-Oriented Study of Bald Eagle Concentrations in Glacier National Park" (David S. Shea, M.S. thesis, University of Montana, 1973).

# Nevada

## Stillwater Wildlife Management Area (near Fallon)

**Raptors:** Wintering Bald Eagles.

**Viewing Season:** December through February.

**Description:** Large dead cottonwood trees near open water along Indian Lakes. Also similar habitat along Soda Lakes and Sheckler, Leter, Harmon, Rattlesnake, and Lahontan reservoirs, all of which are located in the nearby Lahontan Valley around Fallon.

**Access:** Each of the sites is reached from Fallon by driving in various directions from the town. The sites are usually located northeast or southwest of Fallon. Inquire locally for more specific directions.

**Reference:** *WMBE.*

# New Mexico

## Maxwell National Wildlife Refuge (near Maxwell)

**Raptors:** Wintering Bald Eagles.

**Viewing Season:** November to March.

**Description:** Refuge areas which are open or exposed such as grassland and old home sites particularly west of Lake 14 and north of Lake 12.

**Access:** From Maxwell drive north on Old U.S. Route 85 to State Route 505. Turn left (west) onto State Route 505 and continue for about 2 miles (3.2 kilometers) to a road leading to the refuge headquarters where additional information is available.

**Reference:** *WMBE.*

# New York

## Basherkill Marsh (near Westbrookville)

**Raptors:** Bald Eagles (maximum 4 per day).

**Viewing Season:** Mid-March to mid-April.

**Description:** An extensive freshwater marsh used regularly by eagles before their spring migrations are begun.

**Access:** From Port Jervis drive north on U.S. Route 209 for about 15 miles (24 kilometers) to the town of Westbrookville. Drive through the town and continue north on Route 209 for about 2 miles (3.2 kilometers), then turn right onto the first asphalt road which takes you to the marsh. Alternatively from Exit 113 of State Route 17 near the village of Wurtsboro drive south on U.S. Route 209 for about 2 miles (3.2 kilometers), then turn left onto the first asphalt road which also leads to the marsh. Observe from suitable spots around the marsh. Do not attempt to approach eagles closely.

**Reference:** *Birding,* 1977, 9 (6).264s–264t.

## Rondout Reservoir (near Ellenville)

**Raptors:** Wintering Bald Eagles.

**Viewing Season:** Mid-December to mid-March.

**Description:** Either of two state roads closely paralleling the shoreline of the reservoir. Eagles perch in trees along the shoreline of the reservoir at the northwest end, or fish in open water at the nearby power plant.

**Access:** From Ellenville drive north on U.S. Route 209 to the junction with State Route 55. Turn left (northwest) onto Route 55 at the village of Napanoch and drive for about 5 miles (8 kilometers) to a Y junction of State Routes 55 and 55A. Take either route and drive along the reservoir shoreline looking for eagles at the northwest end. *Warning:* Do not attempt to approach eagles on foot. There are severe state and federal penalties for molesting these birds.

**Reference:** None.

# Oklahoma

## Salt Plains National Wildlife Refuge

**Raptors:** Concentrations of Golden Eagles and Bald Eagles.
**Viewing Season:** Winter months.
**Description:** A 32,000-acre wildlife refuge consisting of marshes, ponds, and fields.
**Access:** From the town of Jet drive north on State Route 38 to a point 2 miles (3.2 kilometers) south of the junction of Routes 38 and 11, then turn west for a mile (1.6 kilometers) to the refuge headquarters. Signs direct visitors to the refuge. Secure eagle-watching information at the headquarters.
**Reference:** *Salt Plains National Wildlife Refuge, Oklahoma* (U.S. Fish and Wildlife Service, 1976).

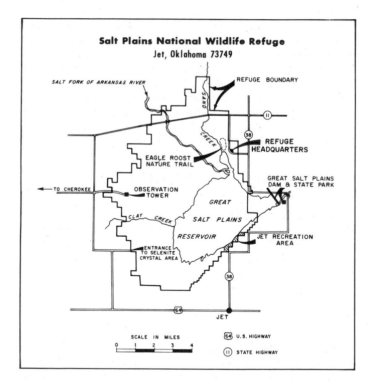

# Pennsylvania

## Pymatuning Waterfowl Area (near Linesville)

**Raptors:** Nesting Bald Eagles.
**Viewing Season:** Spring and summer.
**Description:** Large dead trees in the vicinity of the Pennsylvania Game Commission's waterfowl museum on Ford Island.
**Access:** From Linesville drive south on an unnumbered road to the waterfowl museum on Ford Island where full information is available on eagle viewing.
**Reference:** *Birds of the Pymatuning Region* (Pennsylvania Game Commission, 1952).

# South Dakota

## Fort Randall Dam (near Pickstown)

**Raptors:** Large concentrations of Bald Eagles. Ferruginous Hawks and Golden Eagles are also seen along with lesser numbers of Sharp-shinned Hawks, Red-tailed Hawks, Rough-legged Hawks, Northern Harriers, and American Kestrels.
**Viewing Season:** November through March, particularly late December and early January for Bald Eagles.
**Description:** Areas immediately below the Fort Randall Dam including a tree some 100 feet (30 meters) from the Powerhouse Road, trees on the east bank adjacent to the Spillway Road, large trees on the west bank near the Randall Creek Campground, and the tailraces visible from Tailrace Road.
**Access:** From Pickstown drive south for a short distance to the dam. Stop at the Corps of Engineers Ranger Station for additional information and maps of the area, then continue to the previously mentioned spots.
**Reference:** "The Ecology of Wintering Bald Eagles in Southeastern South Dakota" (Karen Steenhof, M.S. thesis, University of Missouri, Columbia, Missouri).

# Tennessee

## Cross Creeks National Wildlife Refuge (near Dover)

**Raptors:** Small numbers of wintering Bald Eagles.
**Viewing Season:** Winter months.
**Description:** A 9,892-acre refuge consisting of Barkley Lake and sections of the Cumberland River, ponds, marshes, and fields.
**Access:** From Dover drive east on State Route 49 for about 2 miles (3.2 kilometers), then continue north for about 1 mile (1.6 kilometers) on a county road. Signs point to the refuge.
**Reference:** *GBF.*

## Reelfoot Lake State Park and Reelfoot National Wildlife Refuge (near Tiptonville)

**Raptors:** Concentrations of wintering Bald Eagles.

**Viewing Season:** November to mid-March; largest numbers of eagles (up to 100 per day) usually are seen in January and February.

**Description:** A large lake with islands, wooded swamps, and other aquatic habitats. Eagles occur anywhere at the lake, especially along the shoreline and soaring over open water.

**Access:** From the town of Tiptonville follow Routes 21 and 22 around the lake keeping watch for eagles aloft or along the shoreline. Formal eagle-viewing tours are organized by naturalists at Reelfoot State Park daily and on weekends in winter. The tours depart from Airpark Inn. Guest lecturers also present special programs at the Inn on Friday and Saturday evenings during the eagle-viewing season. For details contact the naturalist at Reelfoot Lake State Park, Tiptonville, Tenn. 38079.

**References:** *WMBE; GBF.*

# Utah

## Bear River Migratory Bird Refuge (near Brigham City)

**Raptors:** Wintering Bald Eagles (up to 125 reported per day).

**Viewing Season:** Early November to April with peak numbers being seen in early December and again in February and March.

**Description:** Ice floes and open water channels where carp gather along the refuge's tour route.

**Access:** From Brigham City drive west for about 15 miles (24 kilometers) to the refuge headquarters at which point the 12-mile-long (19.2 kilometers) tour route through the refuge begins. Register at the headquarters before beginning the tour.

**Reference:** *WMBE.*

## Pelican Lake (near Vernal)

**Raptors:** Wintering Golden Eagles and Bald Eagles.

**Viewing Season:** November and March.

**Description:** The shorelines of Pelican Lake or open water areas during periods of freezing.

**Access:** From Vernal drive west on Highway 40 to the junction with State Highway 88, then continue south on Highway 88 for 7 miles (11.2 kilometers) to a stop sign. Pelican Lake is located ahead of you. Continue left (south) on Highway 88 for another 2 miles (3.2 kilometers) to the east end of the lake. Check the surrounding area with binoculars for eagles from this point. Continue to another road joining from the north by driving right for

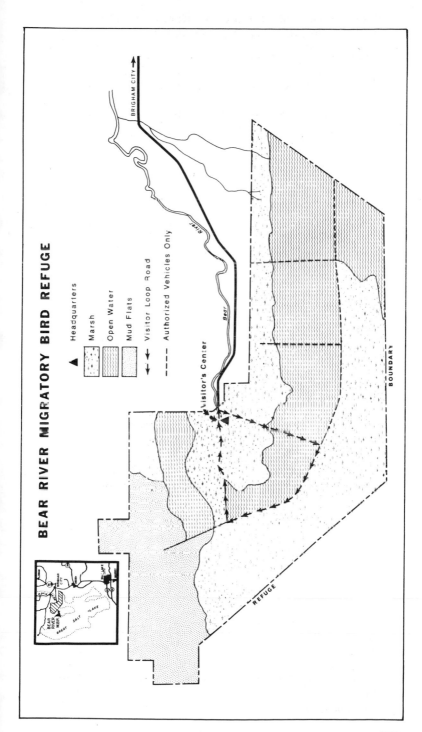

# BEAR RIVER MIGRATORY BIRD REFUGE

▲ Headquarters

Marsh

Open Water

Mud Flats

→← Visitor Loop Road

--- Authorized Vehicles Only

Visitor's Center

Bear River

BRIGHAM CITY

REFUGE BOUNDARY

about 100 yards (90 meters) from the stop sign. Then continue south (left) on the road which leads to other roads around Pelican Lake. Approach the lake from various directions looking for eagles while en route.

**Reference:** *WMBE.*

## Willard Canyon Bald Eagle Roost

**Raptors:** Concentrations of Bald Eagles (up to 100 per day).

**Viewing Season:** Mid-November to late March, with the best eagle viewing from late February to mid-March.

**Description:** Dense stands of Douglas fir on the 6,000- to 9,000-foot (1,800 to 2,700 meter) slopes of rugged Willard Canyon. Eagle watchers should always exercise great caution and restraint. Watch the birds from safe distances to avoid disturbing them at their roost sites. The best eagle-viewing opportunities can be enjoyed during the afternoon and early evening before sunset.

**Access:** From the junction of Routes 89–91 and 69 at the southern end of Brigham City, drive south on Route 89 for 6 miles (9.6 kilometers) to the town of Willard. Turn left (east) onto 200 South Street and drive through the town. Continue on the paved road (1 mile [1.6 kilometers] or less) as it winds northeastward toward the mouth of Willard Canyon. Park along the side of the road at a creek bed. Then hike up the narrow portion of the canyon, or observe from the bench region (an elevated area) just north of the mouth of the canyon. Observe from there.

**Reference:** *Wilson Bulletin,* 1964, 76 (2):186–87.

# Washington

## North Cascades National Park Service Complex

**Raptors:** Wintering Bald Eagles.

**Viewing Season:** Late October to mid-March, with the largest numbers of eagles appearing in late December and January.

**Description:** The shoreline of the Skagit River in the western corridor of North Cascades National Park Complex and portions of the river just west of the park. *Warning:* There are severe federal and state penalties for molesting eagles. Do not approach them closely.

**Access:** From the junction of Interstate 5 and State Route 20 at Burlington, drive east on State Route 20 to North Cascades National Park. This road parallels the Skagit River for some 43 miles (68.8 kilometers) and provides good eagle-viewing opportunities at various locations along the river. See also the site information for the Skagit River Bald Eagle Natural Area.

**References:** *WMBE; Washington Wildlife,* 1977, 29 (3):9–13.

# Olympic National Park

**Raptors:** Wintering Bald Eagles.
**Viewing Season:** Mid-November to late February.
**Description:** An unusually wild and scenic ocean coastline along the Olympic Peninsula, especially between Rialto Beach and Cape Alava where an average of one eagle has been reported for every 500 meters of coastline; also the shorelines of the Bogachiel, Hoh, Queets, and Quinault rivers which flow westward from the Olympic Mountains into the Pacific Ocean.
**Access:** Various routes can be followed for visiting the sites just mentioned.

*Rialto Beach*—From Forks drive north on U.S. Route 101 for about 2 miles (3.2 kilometers), then turn left (west) onto the county road leading to Mora. This road also leads to Rialto Beach.

*Cape Alava*—From Port Angeles drive west on State Route 112 for about 53 miles (84.8 kilometers), then turn southwest on the Ozette Road and follow it for another 20 miles (32 kilometers) to the Lake Ozette Ranger Station. From there walk for about 3 miles (4.8 kilometers) to Cape Alava. *Caution:* When hiking the beaches in winter be alert for weather changes which frequently bring gales and severe drops in temperatures. Particular care should also be taken to avoid being trapped between headland cliffs and incoming tides which provide no escape. Always consult local tide schedules before attempting to hike long distances on the beach.

*Rivers*—Those flowing into the Pacific Ocean within the park can be reached by driving north or south on U.S. Route 101 and turning east or west as appropriate for visiting eagle-watching sites at river shorelines.
**References:** *WMBE.*

# San Juan Island National Historic Park

**Raptors:** Bald Eagles; also 17 other species of raptors.
**Viewing Season:** Mid-November through late February with the largest numbers of Bald Eagles being seen in mid-January. Some eagles also can be seen during other seasons.
**Description:** Open grassland around the American Camp Unit bounded by forest and sea coast.
**Access:** From Anacortes, Washington, or Sidney, British Columbia, board the Washington State Ferry and cross to San Juan Island. At the island town of Friday Harbor drive south on a well-marked county road for 6.25 miles (10 kilometers) to the park's American Camp Unit where Bald Eagles can be observed. Eagle watching can be enjoyed on other sections of the island as well. The island also can be reached by airplane and private boat.

**References:** *WMBE; Washington Wildlife,* 1977, 29 (3):9–13.

## Skagit River Bald Eagle Natural Area

**Raptors:** Large numbers (maximum 160 per day) of wintering Bald Eagles feeding on carcasses of spawned-out salmon.

**Viewing Season:** Late October to mid-March, with the largest numbers of birds appearing in late December and January.

**Description:** A 1,500-acre refuge in northwestern Washington located along a 7-mile-long (11.2 kilometers) protected corridor of the Skagit River between Rockport and Marblemount. Eagle viewing and other activities are permitted on the north bank of the river but prohibited on the south bank where eagles normally feed because the birds are extremely sensitive to human disturbance. Under no circumstances should anyone attempt to float down the river to the eagle feeding area during the critical feeding months of December and January because such activity has serious effects on the feeding behavior of the birds.

**Access:** From Rockport drive northeast on Route 20 along the Skagit River to either of two eagle-viewing sites where the road is close to the north bank of the river. Watch from these sites but do not attempt to approach the birds. For additional information write to The Skagit Eagle Natural Area Manager, P.O. Box 102, Rockport, Wash. 98283.

**References:** *WMBE; Washington Wildlife,* 1977, 29 (3):9–13.

# Wisconsin

## Cassville

**Raptors:** Bald Eagles.

**Viewing Season:** Winter.

**Description:** Open water near the town's Upper Power Plant or the Mississippi River shoreline near the hotel.

**Access:** In Cassville ask directions to the Upper Power Plant. Drive there and park near the plant, but remain in your car to avoid disturbing the eagles feeding in open water nearby. Alternatively drive to the hotel, park on the other side of the railroad tracks, and look for eagles along the river shoreline.

**Reference:** *WBMR.*

## Genoa to Prairie Du Chien Area

**Raptors:** Bald Eagles.

**Viewing Season:** Late November to early December, or late February to early March.

**Description:** Bluffs along State Route 35 and the nearby Mississippi River over which eagles soar.

**Access:** From Genoa drive toward Prairie du Chien (or vice versa) along State Route 35. Watch for eagles soaring along the nearby bluffs.

**Reference:** *WBMR.*

## Mississippi Lock and Dam 4 (near Alma)

**Raptors:** Bald Eagles.

**Viewing Season:** Early winter and mid-March.

**Description:** Open areas of the Mississippi River or along bluffs near the highway between Fountain City and Alma.

**Access:** From Alma drive south on State Route 35 toward Fountain City. Look for eagles along or over the nearby river, or birds flying over nearby bluffs.

**Reference:** *WBMR.*

## Nelson Dewey State Park (near Cassville)

**Raptors:** Bald Eagles and Red-shouldered Hawks.

**Viewing Season:** Winter.

**Description:** A drive-in lookout overlooking the Mississippi River. Observers can look down upon eagles feeding along the river or perched in trees nearby. Red-shouldered Hawks are sometimes seen in trees north of the park's parking lot.

**Access:** From Cassville drive north on Route 133 for a short distance, then turn onto County Route V V. Continue north on this road for 5 miles (8 kilometers) or more until you reach the park (which may be closed at certain times). Enter and drive to the lookout from which eagle watching can be enjoyed.

**Reference:** *WBMR.*

# Canada

Bald Eagles are exceptionally abundant raptors in British Columbia with about 10,000 pairs scattered throughout the province, especially along the coast. There are many locations where these birds can be observed. Most of those discussed here are easy to visit and are noted for large numbers of eagles.

## Active Pass (in the Gulf Islands)

**Raptors:** Bald Eagles.
**Viewing Season:** October to July.
**Description:** The vicinity of Helen Point at the southeastern end of Active Pass as well as the southside of the pass. Eagles also circling over the western end of the pass and adjacent mountains can be seen with binoculars.
**Access:** Active Pass is located in the Gulf Islands between Mayne and Galiano islands. The area can be visited by riding the British Columbia Government ferries between Vancouver or Tsawwassen and Victoria at Swartz Bay. Observers should stand on the ferry bow or starboard for the best eagle-viewing opportunities.
**Reference:** *Adventure with Eagles* (Hancock House, 1970).

## Fraser Valley (northeast of Vancouver)

**Raptors:** Bald Eagles (up to 100 per day).
**Viewing Season:** October to January.
**Description:** The shorelines of the Harrison and Pitt rivers in the Fraser Valley.
**Access:** Via automobile on a well-routed highway (marked on local British Columbia maps) up the Fraser Valley.
**Reference:** None.

## Pacific Rim National Park (on Vancouver Island)

**Raptors:** Nesting Bald Eagles (over 170 pairs in a 400-square-mile area).
**Viewing Season:** Spring, summer, and autumn.
**Description:** The islands and shorelines of Barkley Sound.
**Access:** By private boat from the towns of Ucluelet or Bamfield. Ucluelet can be reached by automobile via Route 4 on Vancouver Island. Private airplane charters from Vancouver and Victoria can also transport visitors to Barkley Sound in the park.
**Reference:** *Adventure with Eagles* (Hancock House, 1970).

## Prince Rupert

**Raptors:** Bald Eagles.
**Viewing Season:** All year.
**Description:** The area around the harbor or the Prince Rupert garbage dump where from 5 to 40 eagles feed.
**Access:** By ferry or automobile on Canada Route 16.
**Reference:** None.

# Other Raptor Viewing Areas

## California

### Dough Flat Condor Observation Site (near Fillmore)

**Raptors:** Turkey Vulture, California Condor, Golden Eagle.
**Viewing Season:** February through April.
**Description:** An area marked "Dough Flat" providing a view of cliffs to the east where California Condors are sometimes seen early in the morning or late in the afternoon. Dough Flat is part of the public access corridor within the Sespe Condor Sanctuary.
**Access:** From Los Angeles drive north on Interstate 5 (Golden State Freeway) for 33 miles (52.8 kilometers) to Castaic Junction. Leave the Freeway at the Ventura off-ramp and follow State Route 126 for 19 miles (30.4 kilometers) to Fillmore. At a traffic light on A Street (which eventually becomes Goodenough Road) turn right and continue north for 3 miles (4.8 kilometers). Then turn right onto an oiled road (you will arrive at a locked gate if you pass this oiled road) and follow it for about 5 miles (8 kilometers) to a junction with a sign marked "Oil Fields and Condor Observation Site." Keep left and continue past another major junction (ignoring several small roads leading off the main road) to the Dough Flat parking area. Park and follow a short trail to the top of a low hill from which one can sometimes observe condors. There is a 40 percent possibility of seeing condors here in winter, and a 50 percent possibility of seeing them in spring. For your best chances of seeing the birds you should arrive by 9:30 A.M. and remain on the post until 4:00 P.M. Early morning and late afternoon are the most likely periods when condors are seen.

Camping can be done nearby at the Cow Spring campground (about 3 miles [4.8 kilometers] from Dough Flat) that is reached by driving past Dough Flat and continuing to the campground. You must supply your own water.

Occasionally roads are washed out following winter storms thus making it necessary to check on road conditions by telephoning the Ojai Ranger Station at 805-646-4348 before entering the area. For additional information contact the National Audubon Society Condor Naturalist, 2208 Sunridge Drive, Ventura, Calif. 93003.
**Reference:** *Birding,* 1978, 10 (1):1–5.

### Edminston Pump Plant Condor Observation Point (near Grapevine)

**Raptors:** California Condors.

**Viewing Season:** October.

**Description:** A parking lot (Visitors Overlook) from which one looks down at a water pumping station and over dry grassland flats toward the north, and grassy hills toward the south. Condor watchers should make slow, careful searches of the surrounding area looking for condors feeding, perching, or flying overhead. *Warning:* Do not walk from the parking lot or nearby roadside onto private ranchland. Persons doing so will be arrested. Ranchers are providing safe feeding and roosting areas for condors, and these birds are *never* to be approached or molested. Persons looking for condors should arrive at this site by 9:00 A.M. and be prepared to remain at least until 4:00 P.M. There is an 85 percent possibility of seeing condors here.

**Access:** From Los Angeles drive north on Interstate 5 (Golden State Freeway) through Castaic Junction and Gorman (buy gasoline there while looking overhead for condors) and over the Tejon Pass to the Grapevine exit on the Freeway. Leave the Freeway there and look for a road leading eastward marked "Edminston Pump Plant." Follow this road for about 8 miles (12.8 kilometers) to the parking lot and Visitors Overlook (the site is surrounded by a chain-link fence). Park here and look for condors. If the parking lot gate is closed, backtrack along the road stopping at high spots from which good views of condors in the distance are possible.

**Reference:** *Birding,* 1978, 10 (1):1–5.

## Hunt-Wesson Hawk and Owl Preserve (near Davis)

**Raptors:** Abundant—Red-tailed Hawk, White-tailed Kite, American Kestrel, and Northern Harrier. Common—Rough-legged Hawk, Barn Owl, and Short-eared Owl. Uncommon—Ferruginous Hawk, Great Horned Owl, and Burrowing Owl. Rare—Prairie Falcon and Merlin.

**Viewing Season:** Late October to March.

**Description:** A 320-acre area consisting of undulating ditches and cropland on which a series of sprinkler heads spray food processing waste water. The sprinkler heads are used as hunting and feeding perches by the raptors.

**Access:** From Davis drive east on Route 80 to the Mace Boulevard exit. Take this exit and drive north on Mace Boulevard until it curves to the west and becomes Covell Boulevard. Remain on Covell Boulevard until you arrive at the stop sign at Road 102. Turn right onto Road 102 and follow it north for about 3 miles (4.8 kilometers) to Road 28H. Turn right and continue east on Road 28H to the preserve located about a mile (1.6 kilometers) down the road on the north side. A fence prevents access to the property, and it is marked by a sign reading "Hawk and Owl Preserve—sponsored by Hunt-Wesson Foods, Inc." However, observation of raptors is easy and can be done by parking along Road 28H or on another road running along the eastern border of the preserve.

**Reference:** *Audubon Leader,* 1977, 18 (9):4.


## Mt. Pinos Condor Observation Point (near Lake-of-the-Woods)

**Raptors:** Turkey Vulture, California Condor, Golden Eagle.

**Viewing Season:** July and August. August is the most productive month.

**Description:** The summit of Mt. Pinos (elevation 8,833 feet or 2,650 meters) from which observers have excellent views of surrounding slopes and mountains above which condors are sometimes observed. Occasionally the birds approach within 100 feet (30 meters) of observers. When looking for the birds, scan the horizon, rock faces, and dead tree snags for them. Also make occasional searches overhead. *Warning:* Birders and photographers should not run or quickly approach condors when they land on nearby trees since such movements may cause them to move to other perches. There are severe state penalties for harassment of California Condors. Violators of condor protection laws will be dealt with to the full extent of the law.

**Access:** From Los Angeles drive north on Interstate 5 (Golden State Freeway) for 64 miles (102.4 kilometers) through the town of Gorman and over the Tejon Pass to the Frazier Park off-ramp. This is the first off-ramp north of Gorman. Exit here and drive west for 6.8 miles (10.8 kilometers) through Frazier Park to Lake-of-the-Woods. When the road forks, follow the right fork and continue up Mt. Pinos road for 19 miles (30.4 kilometers). Ignore a junction with a right turn on the road. Instead, remain on the main road past the McGill and Mt. Pinos campgrounds (both excellent) to a large parking area where the road ends. Enter the parking area, then follow an unpaved road leading off the left side of the parking area for 1.5 miles (2.4 kilometers) to the paved parking lot at the condor observation point. Park here, then walk along a short trail to the benches at the Mt. Pinos Condor Observation Point. There is a 60 percent possibility of seeing condors at this Point. For additional information contact the National Audubon Society Condor Naturalist, 2208 Sunridge Drive, Ventura, Calif. 93003.

**Reference:** *Birding,* 1978, 10 (1):1–5.


# Florida

## Everglades National Park (near Homestead)

**Raptors:** Turkey Vulture, Black Vulture, Swallow-tailed Kite,

Red-shouldered Hawk, Short-tailed Hawk, Bald Eagle, Osprey, and American Kestrel.

**Viewing Season:** November through March.

**Description:** A 2,100-square-mile segment of the Everglades containing hammocks, saw-grass marshes, sloughs, wet prairies, and bays. Raptors are likely to be seen almost anywhere within the park, but birders seeking the rare Short-tailed Hawk should devote particular attention to the area between West Lake (mile 30.5 or kilometer 48.8 from the park entrance) and Flamingo along the road traversing the park. A map is available at the park information center.

**Access:** From Homestead drive south and west on State Route 27 following well-marked directional signs to the park entrance.

**References:** *GEHW; GBF; A Guide to Everglades National Park and the Nearby Florida Keys* (Golden Press, 1960).

## Loxahatchee National Wildlife Refuge

**Raptors:** Turkey Vulture, Black Vulture, Osprey, Swallow-tailed Kite, Snail Kite, Sharp-shinned Hawk, Cooper's Hawk, Red-tailed Hawk, Red-shouldered Hawk, Broad-winged Hawk, Short-tailed Hawk, Bald Eagle, Northern Harrier, Peregrine Falcon, Merlin, and American Kestrel.

**Viewing Season:** All year.

**Description:** A 145,635-acre refuge containing portions of the Everglades, saw-grass marsh, wet prairies, tree islands, and sloughs.

**Access:** From the junction of U.S. Route 1 and State Route 80 near West Palm Beach drive west on Route 80 to the junction with U.S. Route 441. Turn onto Route 441 and drive south for several miles to the refuge entrance road.

**Reference:** *GBF.*

# Idaho

## Snake River Birds of Prey Natural Area (near Boise)

**Raptors:** Turkey Vulture, Osprey, Cooper's Hawk, Red-tailed Hawk, Swainson's Hawk, Rough-legged Hawk, Ferruginous Hawk, Golden Eagle, Bald Eagle, Northern Harrier, Prairie Falcon, Peregrine Falcon, and American Kestrel. Also various species of owls.

**Viewing Season:** All seasons, but particularly during spring, summer, and autumn.

**Description:** A unique 31,000-acre natural area containing rugged river canyons and cliffs which provide nest sites for large numbers of hawks, eagles, and falcons along 33 miles (52.8 kilometers) of the Snake River in southwestern Idaho. The area is

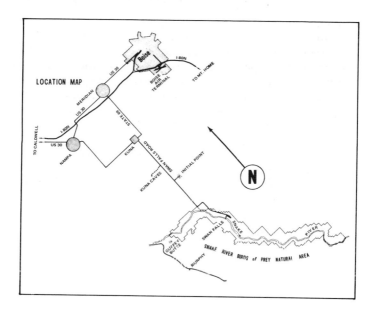

LOCATION MAP

noted for impressive numbers of nesting Golden Eagles and Prairie Falcons.

**Access:** From Boise, Idaho, drive west on U.S. Route 30 to Meridan, then continue south on State Route 69 to Kuna. From Kuna drive south for about 18 miles (28.8 kilometers) on the Swan Falls Road to Swan Falls within the Birds of Prey Natural Area. Various roads also run through the area. Circulars and maps, along with additional information, are available from the Manager, Birds of Prey Natural Area, Bureau of Land Management, 230 Collins Road, Boise, Idaho 83702.

**References:** *Snake River Birds of Prey Research Project Annual Report* (U.S. Department of the Interior, Bureau of Land Management, 1975, 1976).

# Texas

## Santa Ana National Wildlife Refuge

**Raptors:** Turkey Vulture, Black Vulture, Osprey, White-tailed Kite, Swallow-tailed Kite, Mississippi Kite, Hook-billed Kite, Sharp-shinned Hawk, Cooper's Hawk, Red-tailed Hawk, Red-shouldered Hawk, Broad-winged Hawk, Swainson's Hawk, Zone-tailed Hawk, White-tailed Hawk, Gray Hawk, Harris' Hawk, Common Black Hawk, Northern Harrier, Crested Caracara, Prairie Falcon, Peregrine Falcon, Merlin, and American Kestrel.

**Viewing Season:** All months.

**Description:** Subtropical forest, lakes, and marshes covering 1,980 acres along the Rio Grande River.

**Access:** From McAllen drive south on 10th Street (which becomes Route 336) for about 6 miles (9.6 kilometers) to the junction with U.S. Route 281 (Old Military Road). Turn left (east) onto U.S. Route 281 and continue for another 10 miles (16 kilometers) toward Brownsville. Then look for the refuge sign along the right side of the highway. Turn right and drive into the refuge. Literature and information can be secured at the headquarters.

**Reference:** *A Birder's Guide to the Rio Grande Valley of Texas* (L & P Photography, 1971).

# Appendix 1

# Accidental North American Raptor Sightings

In addition to the species described earlier in this guide, a few others have been observed accidentally in North America. These are birds of prey which are vagrants. They occurred here unexpectedly far from their normal geographic ranges or at the extreme limit of their ranges. They probably will not occur here again or, if they do, only at infrequent intervals.

## King Vulture *Sarcoramphus papa*

Central and South American species noted along St. Johns River in Florida in 1774 and 1775 (*A.O.U. Check-List*, 1957:100).

## Roadside Hawk *Buteo magnirostris*

Recorded once in 1901 in Cameron County, Texas.

## Steller's Sea Eagle *Haliaeetus pelagicus*

Three Alaska records: May 1906 on Unalaska (eastern Aleutians); 1917 on St. Paul Island (Pribilofs); 1921 on Kodiak Island.

## Kestrel *Falco tinnunculus*

This Old World falcon resembling the American Kestrel occurred in eastern North America on two occasions. On 29 September 1887 female was collected near Nantasket, Massachusetts; on 23 September 1972 another individual was trapped at a banding station at Cape May Point, New Jersey. The New Jersey bird had oil on its feathers suggesting it may have been transported on board a ship off the New Jersey coast. One record for this species was collected 9 December 1959 on Martinique, West Indies.

# Appendix 2

# Hawks of the Hawaiian Islands

Only one species of hawk is native to the Hawaiian Islands, the endangered Hawaiian Hawk or Io, although occasionally a few other species have been reported from some of the islands as vagrants. The material in this appendix is based largely upon information published by Andrew J. Berger (*Hawaiian Birdlife,* 1972) supplemented by newly published and unpublished information.

## Hawaiian Hawk (Io) *Buteo solitarius*

**Wingspread:** Information unavailable.
**Length:** 15½ to 18 inches (39.3 to 45.6 centimeters).
**Field Recognition:** Endangered. Small, chunky soaring hawk occurs in two (perhaps three) color phases. *Adult (dark phase)*— Dark blackish-brown on upperparts and undersides. *Adult (light phase)*—Head and neck tawny or buffy fading to white in worn plumage; upperparts dark brown, throat and undersides whitish or washed rust. Eyes brown. Bill black with basal portion bluish. Legs and feet greenish-yellow. *Immature (dark phase)*—Dark blackish-brown above, dark brown or blackish below with tawny mottling and obscure bars. *Immature (light phase)*—Sides of head and back dark brown, underparts whitish to buffy with streaks formed by brown blotches on breast. This may be third adult color phase. Matter subject to additional study.
**Flight Style:** Soars over mountain gullies and slopes. Stoops during courtship displays.
**Voice:** *Kee-oh* or *i-o;* "squeaking" sound (Brown and Amadon).
**Nest:** Large stick structure placed high in tree.
**Eggs:** 2 or 3 (subject to verification) possibly light blue. Incubation period unknown.
**Food:** Mostly rats and mice but formerly insects. Occasionally birds or other prey taken.
**Habitat:** Frequently perches on limbs of trees in parkland with scattering of large trees, forested edges of fields, natural clearings among forests at elevations between 2,000 and 8,500 feet (600 and 2,550 meters).

**Range:** Endemic to Island of Hawaii where few hundred survive. In field study conducted in 1967 and 1968 (see *Elepaio,* 1969, 29:75–79), 62 hawks were observed during about 1,200 hours of observation (0.05 hawks per hour). Recently seen on slopes of Mauna Loa (windward and Kona coasts), Mauna Kea (uncommon), and in Hawaii Volcanoes National Park. Occasionally seen elsewhere on island. Noted once (28 September 1977) on Oahu shortly after volcanic eruption on Hawaii.

## Osprey *Pandion haliaetus*

**Hawaiian Islands Distribution:** Observed in 1939, 1940, 1949, 1955, 1956, 1968, 1970, 1971, and 1977 on Oahu; in 1969 on Kauai; in 1977 on Maui.

## Golden Eagle *Aquila chrysaetos*

**Hawaiian Islands Distribution:** One bird observed on 19 May 1967, August 1967, September 1967, January 1969, and 5 May 1977 in Waimea Canyon, Kauai.

## Steller's Sea Eagle *Haliaeetus pelagicus*

**Hawaiian Islands Distribution:** One bird observed and photographed in February 1978 on Kure Atoll.

## Northern Harrier (Marsh Hawk) *Circus cyaneus*

**Hawaiian Islands Distribution:** Reported in 1900s on Oahu; in 1964 on Midway Atoll.

## Peregrine Falcon *Falco peregrinus*

**Hawaiian Islands Distribution:** Observed in 1961 in Hawaii Volcanoes National Park, Hawaii; in November 1965, December 1966, January 1968, December 1968 and 1976, March 1977 on Oahu; December 1975 and January 1976 on Kauai; in 1965 on Lisianski Island; in 1967 on Midway Atoll; and in 1965 on Kure Atoll.

## American Kestrel *Falco sparverius*

**Hawaiian Islands Distribution:** Observed from January to March 1970 at Fort Shafter, Oahu.

# Appendix 3

# Raptor Conservation Organizations

In addition to the well-known national conservation organizations, all of which support the protection and conservation of birds of prey, the following organizations are especially concerned with raptor conservation.

Eagle Valley Environmentalists, Inc.
P. O. Box 155
Apple River, Ill. 61001

Hawk Migration Association of North America
c/o Hawk Mountain Sanctuary
R.D. 2
Kempton, Pa. 19529

Hawk Mountain Sanctuary Association
R.D. 2
Kempton, Pa. 19529

International Council for Bird Preservation
c/o Smithsonian Institution
Washington, D.C. 20560

New Paltz Peregrine Falcon Foundation, Inc.
10 Joalyn Road
New Paltz, N.Y. 12561

The Peregrine Fund
Cornell Laboratory of Ornithology
159 Sapsucker Woods Road
Ithaca, N.Y. 14853

Raptor Information Center
National Wildlife Federation
1412 Sixteenth Street, N.W.
Washington, D.C. 20036

Raptor Research Foundation, Inc.
c/o Department of Zoology
Brigham Young University
Provo, Utah 84602

Society for the Preservation of Birds of Prey
Box 891
Pacific Palisades, Calif. 90272

Southwest Hawk Watch
4619 East Arcadia Lane
Phoenix, Arizona 85018

# Appendix 4

# Field Data Forms

**HAWK MIGRATION DATA SHEET**

Date: _____ Observers: _____

Location: _____

| | 7-8 | 8-9 | 9-10 | 10-11 | 11-12 | 12-1 | 1-2 | 2-3 | 3-4 | 4-5 | 5-6 | 6-7 | Totals |
|---|---|---|---|---|---|---|---|---|---|---|---|---|---|
| Time (E.S.T.) | | | | | | | | | | | | | |
| Max. Vis. (Miles) | | | | | | | | | | | | | |
| Air Temp. | | | | | | | | | | | | | |
| Wind Speed (MPH) | | | | | | | | | | | | | |
| Wind Direction | | | | | | | | | | | | | |
| % Cloud Cover | | | | | | | | | | | | | |
| Turkey Vulture | | | | | | | | | | | | | |
| Goshawk | | | | | | | | | | | | | |
| Sharp-shinned Hawk | | | | | | | | | | | | | |
| Cooper's Hawk | | | | | | | | | | | | | |
| Red-tailed Hawk | | | | | | | | | | | | | |
| Red-shouldered Hawk | | | | | | | | | | | | | |
| Broad-winged Hawk | | | | | | | | | | | | | |
| Rough-legged Hawk | | | | | | | | | | | | | |
| Golden Eagle | | | | | | | | | | | | | |
| Bald Eagle | | | | | | | | | | | | | |
| Marsh Hawk | | | | | | | | | | | | | |
| Osprey | | | | | | | | | | | | | |
| Peregrine Falcon | | | | | | | | | | | | | |
| Pigeon Hawk | | | | | | | | | | | | | |
| Sparrow Hawk | | | | | | | | | | | | | |
| Unidentified Hawk | | | | | | | | | | | | | |
| Totals | | | | | | | | | | | | | |

NOTES:

# MORNING

Date_____ Area_____ Observers_____

| Time (E.S.T.) | 7-8 | | | 8-9 | | | 9-10 | | | 10-11 | | | 11-12 | | | 12-1 | | | Totals | | |
|---|---|---|---|---|---|---|---|---|---|---|---|---|---|---|---|---|---|---|---|---|---|
| Visibility | | | | | | | | | | | | | | | | | | | | | |
| Air Temp. | | | | | | | | | | | | | | | | | | | | | |
| Bar. Pressure | | | | | | | | | | | | | | | | | | | | | |
| Cloud Cover (%) | | | | | | | | | | | | | | | | | | | | | |
| Wind Direction | | | | | | | | | | | | | | | | | | | | | |
| Wind Velocity | | | | | | | | | | | | | | | | | | | | | |
| | A | I | U | A | I | U | A | I | U | A | I | U | A | I | U | A | I | U | A | I | U |
| Red-tailed | | | | | | | | | | | | | | | | | | | | | |
| Red-shouldered | | | | | | | | | | | | | | | | | | | | | |
| Broad-winged | | | | | | | | | | | | | | | | | | | | | |
| Rough-legged | D | L | U | D | L | U | D | L | U | D | L | U | D | L | U | D | L | U | D | L | U |
| Goshawk | | | | | | | | | | | | | | | | | | | | | |
| Cooper's | | | | | | | | | | | | | | | | | | | | | |
| Sharp-shinned | | | | | | | | | | | | | | | | | | | | | |
| Peregrine | | | | | | | | | | | | | | | | | | | | | |
| Pigeon Hawk | | | | | | | | | | | | | | | | | | | | | |
| Sparrow Hawk | M | F | U | M | F | U | M | F | U | M | F | U | M | F | U | M | F | U | M | F | U |
| Golden Eagle | | | | | | | | | | | | | | | | | | | | | |
| Bald Eagle | | | | | | | | | | | | | | | | | | | | | |
| Osprey | | | | | | | | | | | | | | | | | | | | | |
| Marsh Hawk | | | | | | | | | | | | | | | | | | | | | |
| Unidentified | | | | | | | | | | | | | | | | | | | | | |
| Totals | | | | | | | | | | | | | | | | | | | | | |
| Visitors | | | | | | | | | | | | | | | | | | | | | |

Notes: (PLEASE KEEP RECORDS OF ALL SMALL BIRDS)

275

# AFTERNOON

Date_____ Area_____ Observers_____

| | 1-2 | | | 2-3 | | | 3-4 | | | 4-5 | | | 5-6 | | | 6-7 | | | Totals | | |
|---|---|---|---|---|---|---|---|---|---|---|---|---|---|---|---|---|---|---|---|---|---|
| Time (E.S.T.) | | | | | | | | | | | | | | | | | | | | | |
| Visibility | | | | | | | | | | | | | | | | | | | | | |
| Air Temp. | | | | | | | | | | | | | | | | | | | | | |
| Bar. Pressure | | | | | | | | | | | | | | | | | | | | | |
| Cloud Cover (%) | | | | | | | | | | | | | | | | | | | | | |
| Wind Direction | | | | | | | | | | | | | | | | | | | | | |
| Wind Velocity | | | | | | | | | | | | | | | | | | | | | |
| | A | I | U | A | I | U | A | I | U | A | I | U | A | I | U | A | I | U | A | I | U |
| Red-tailed | | | | | | | | | | | | | | | | | | | | | |
| Red-shouldered | | | | | | | | | | | | | | | | | | | | | |
| Broad-winged | | | | | | | | | | | | | | | | | | | | | |
| | D | L | U | D | L | U | D | L | U | D | L | U | D | L | U | D | L | U | D | L | U |
| Rough-legged | | | | | | | | | | | | | | | | | | | | | |
| Goshawk | | | | | | | | | | | | | | | | | | | | | |
| Cooper's | | | | | | | | | | | | | | | | | | | | | |
| Sharp-shinned | | | | | | | | | | | | | | | | | | | | | |
| Peregrine | | | | | | | | | | | | | | | | | | | | | |
| Pigeon Hawk | | | | | | | | | | | | | | | | | | | | | |
| | M | F | U | M | F | U | M | F | U | M | F | U | M | F | U | M | F | U | M | F | U |
| Sparrow Hawk | | | | | | | | | | | | | | | | | | | | | |
| Golden Eagle | | | | | | | | | | | | | | | | | | | | | |
| Bald Eagle | | | | | | | | | | | | | | | | | | | | | |
| Osprey | | | | | | | | | | | | | | | | | | | | | |
| Marsh Hawk | | | | | | | | | | | | | | | | | | | | | |
| Unidentified | | | | | | | | | | | | | | | | | | | | | |
| Totals | | | | | | | | | | | | | | | | | | | | | |
| Visitors | | | | | | | | | | | | | | | | | | | | | |

Notes: (PLEASE KEEP RECORDS OF ALL SMALL BIRDS)

276

Report by: _____ (a.m. / p.m.)    MONTCLAIR BIRD CLUB - DAILY HAWK COUNT    Date: _____

| Time | Buteos | | | Accipiters | | Falcons | | | Other | | | | Total |
|------|--------|----|----|----|----|------|----|----|----|----|----|----|-------|
| | BW | R- | RS | SS | CH | Sp H | DH | PH | CS | MH | BE | Un | |
| -9 | | | | | | | | | | | | | |
| 9-10 | | | | | | | | | | | | | |
| 10-11 | | | | | | | | | | | | | |
| 11-12 | | | | | | | | | | | | | |
| 12-1 | | | | | | | | | | | | | |
| 1-2 | | | | | | | | | | | | | |
| 2-3 | | | | | | | | | | | | | |
| 3-4 | | | | | | | | | | | | | |
| 4-5 | | | | | | | | | | | | | |
| 5+ | | | | | | | | | | | | | |
| Total | | | | | | | | | | | | | |

# Suggested Reading

Austing, G. Ronald. 1964. *The World of the Red-tailed Hawk*. Philadelphia: J.B. Lippincott

Bent, Arthur Cleveland. 1937. *Life Histories of North American Birds of Prey*. Part 1. United States National Museum Bulletin 167. Reprint. New York: Dover Publications

————1938. *Life Histories of North American Birds of Prey*. Part 2. United States National Museum Bulletin 170. Reprint. New York: Dover Publications

Brett, James J. and Alexander C. Nagy. 1973. *Feathers in the Wind*. Kempton, Pa.: Hawk Mountain Sanctuary Association

Broley, Myrtle Jeanne. 1952. *Eagle Man*. New York: Pellegrini & Cudahy

Broun, Maurice. 1949. *Hawks Aloft: The Story of Hawk Mountain*. New York: Dodd, Mead (out of print)

Brown, Leslie. 1970. *Eagles*. New York: Arco

————1976. *Birds of Prey: Their Biology and Ecology*. New York: A & W Publishers.

————1976. *Eagles of the World*. New York: Universe Books

Brown, Leslie and Dean Amadon. 1968. *Eagles, Hawks and Falcons of the World*. 2 vols. New York: McGraw-Hill

Craighead, John J. and Frank C. Craighead, Jr. 1956. *Hawks, Owls and Wildlife*. Harrisburg, Pa.: Stackpole. Reprint. New York: Dover Publications

Grossman, Mary Louise and John Hamlet. 1964. *Birds of Prey of the World*. New York: Clarkson N. Potter

Hamerstrom, Frances. 1970. *An Eagle to the Sky*. Ames, Iowa: Iowa State University Press

————1972. *Birds of Prey of Wisconsin*. Madison, Wis.: Wisconsin Department of Natural Resources

Harwood, Michael. 1973. *The View from Hawk Mountain*. New York: Scribner's

Hawk Migration Association of North America. 1975. *Proceedings of the North American Hawk Migration Conference 1974*. Washington Depot, Conn.: Shiver Mountain Press (out of print)

Heintzelman, Donald S. 1970. *The Hawks of New Jersey*. New Jersey State Museum Bulletin 13

————1972. *A Guide to Northeastern Hawk Watching*. Lambertville, N.J.: Published Privately (out of print)

————1975. *Autumn Hawk Flights: The Migrations in Eastern North America*. New Brunswick, N.J.: Rutgers University Press

————1976. *A Guide to Eastern Hawk Watching*. University Park, Pa.: Pennsylvania State University Press

————1979. *The Hawks and Owls of North America*. New York: Universe Books

Hickey, Joseph J., ed. 1969. *Peregrine Falcon Populations: Their Biology and Decline*. Madison, Wis.: University of Wisconsin Press

Koford, Carl B. 1953. *The California Condor*. Research Report No. 4. New York: National Audubon Society

Laycock, George. 1973. *Autumn of the Eagle*. New York: Scribner's

Lloyd, Glenys and Derek Lloyd. 1970. *Birds of Prey*. New York: Grosset & Dunlap

May, John Bichard. 1935. *The Hawks of North America*. New York: National Association of Audubon Societies (out of print)

McMillan, Ian. 1968. *Man and the California Condor*. New York: Dutton

Olendorff, Richard R. 1975. *Golden Eagle Country*. New York: Knopf

Porter, R.F., Ian Willis, Steen Christensen, and Bent Pors Nielsen. 1976. *Flight Identification of European Raptors*. 2d. ed. Berkhamsted, England: Poyser

Stone, Witmer. 1937. *Bird Studies at Old Cape May*. 2 vols. Delaware Valley Ornithological Club, Philadelphia, Pa. Reprint. New York: Dover Publications

Wilbur, Sanford R. 1978. "The California Condor, 1966–76: A Look at Its Past and Future." *North American Fauna* 72:1–136.

# Index

Page numbers in boldface type refer to illustrations.